Brief Encounters

Brief Encounters

The Women's Guide to Casual Sex

Emily Dubberley

First published in 2005 by Fusion Press,
a division of Satin Publications Ltd.
101 Southwark Street
London SE1 0JF
UK
info@visionpaperbacks.co.uk
www.visionpaperbacks.co.uk
Publisher: Sheena Dewan

A catalogue record for this book is available from the British Library.

ISBN: 1-904132-66-9

2 4 6 8 10 9 7 5 3 1

Cover and text design by ok?design
Printed and bound in the UK by Mackays of Chatham Ltd,
Chatham, Kent

To Gabrielle Fallopius,
who invented the condom,
thus making casual sex a feasible option

Contents

Acknowledgements

Thanks to:

My grandfather, for inspiring me to write, and my entire family for being supportive rather than getting outraged and disowning me, when I said I was writing a book about casual sex.

All the friends who gave me advice, stories or both; bought me beer and fags when I was too busy writing to leave the house; and distracted me with partying when I got stressed, including (but not limited to) Avril Cooper, Anne Cantelo, Mil Millington, Margret Hotze, Lou Wener, Simon Batistoni, James O'Brien, Emily Rudegirl, Michael Smith, Phil Tipper, Matthew Carrington-Moore, Tom Wright, Rhianna Pratchett, Mark Sloane, Paul Carr, Catherine Morris, Jonathan Oakden, Richard Marr, John Brennan, Steve Lamacq and the entire Punk Rock Karaoke team.

John Handelaar, who helped me create both cliterati.co.uk, which proved I was right about women loving sex, and my personal site, dubberley.com, on which I first mentioned that I wanted to write a sex book and was looking for an agent. Paul Donelley, who read my plea and introduced me to my fab agent, Chelsey Fox. Fusion Press, in particular Charlotte Cole and Emily Bird, for being so easy to deal with as they guided me through writing my first book (and for not changing many words). And everyone who sent me casual sex stories.

The wonderful sexperts who shared their secrets with me: in particular Helen Knox from willyworries.com for great STI info; Robert Page and the whole Lovers' Guide team, Dr Pam Spurr, Flic Everett and Julia Gash.

Gavin Griffiths for letting me write my book, despite the fact that he was paying me to launch *Scarlet* magazine at the same time. And the entire *Scarlet* team – in particular Nahid de Belgeonne, Sarah Hedley and Carolyn Saunders – for not sulking when I turned up late to editorial meetings having got so caught up in writing this that I forgot the time.

Nancy Friday for inspiring me to research and write about sex in the first place.

And, of course, everyone I've ever had a brief encounter with: good, bad and indifferent. Don't worry, I've changed names to protect the not-so-innocent.

Introduction

Most sex, love and relationship manuals are put together on the understanding that everyone is after a long-term relationship; you need an 'other half' to be a whole person. While true love is all very nice, a third of the population is single at any one time. Some people have just come out of long-term relationships. Others have just started university and been confronted with a seething mass of testosterone-packed (or oestrogen-stuffed) humanity to work their way through. Some are so busy with their careers that the idea of maintaining a relationship is anathema; they simply don't have the time. Others are waiting for Mr or Ms Perfect, but in the meantime don't want to be celibate. And some are simply commitment-phobes; a disparaging term but if you're honest about your desire for nothing more than no-strings sex then what's the harm?

This book is for all those people, and anyone else, who, while quite liking the idea of getting laid, isn't entirely sure that they're ready for a full-on, loved-up, monogamous – and possibly libido-sapping – relationship. It covers all the essentials: knowing whether you're able to cope with no-strings fun; stopping yourself from looking (and feeling) desperate; how to pull – and push them out the door without embarrassment the morning after; looking presentable in the office after a hot and unexpected night with a stranger; how to make sure that a sex-packed life doesn't lead to STI-packed pants; dealing with fuck-buddies, one-night stands, bi-curious dabblings, sex with an ex and all other types of brief encounter. And, of course, no sex book would be complete without a section on masturbation. Knowing how to please yourself in the sack is the best way to make sure that you have a good time with other people, so it's well worth devoting time to self-love. Forget diamonds; Jessica Rabbit is a girl's best friend.

When it comes to getting laid, it's sad to say the way that you look will have a massive impact. Confidence goes a long way but add cleavage and you'll probably get further. With this in mind, there's advice on how to go from grim to gorgeous without breaking the bank. It's amazing how effective a few body language tricks can be – and even more amazing what a gel bra can do for a girl's pulling chances.

Being a sex manual, this book's also stuffed with info on what to do once you get your object of desire into the sack. Forget being patronised with explanations of how to get into the missionary position. This book has all the advice you really need; what to do if your date's a crap kisser, dealing with a bloke with a tiny tool or huge horn, how to make sure you're the best fuck your partner's ever had, dealing with someone whose kinks are too out there for you, and how to introduce your own preferences without scaring the horses (as long as you don't actually want horses involved – it's illegal after all). There's advice on how to do all the dirtiest things you've ever imagined, whether foreplay or fantasy. And while cheating – or having sex with someone else's man – is something that you really shouldn't do, it sometimes happens, so you can discover the common pitfalls, along with tips on how to manage as a mistress or avoid getting caught if you fancy a bit of loving on the side.

Being a single bird about town, things can sometimes go wrong, so this book also covers the essentials of getting out of dangerous situations; avoiding drink-spiking, getting away from a man who won't respect your limits and coping with the horror of waking up in an unfamiliar bed in an unfamiliar area with no idea of how to get home – then discovering the man in question has left for work and double-locked the door …

Of course, no matter how much of a modern woman you are, there's always a chance that your heart will get involved, so you can also find out whether it's worth falling for the man you're getting it on with, when it's the right time to use the 'L' word and get tips on avoiding getting your heart broken.

It is possible to live happily ever after with the person of your dreams. But going solo or juggling a man-harem will make you far happier than settling for someone who's not quite right for you. So grab your condoms and get ready for the ride(s) of your life.

Chapter 1

Are Brief Encounters for You?

If you believe what you see on TV and read in women's mags, it's easy to assume that everyone is having casual sex; or, if they're not, then they should be. Going out on the pull is an obligatory part of single life and, by the time most people reach 30, they've got at least one 'waking up in a strange bed' story; frequently involving excessive amounts of alcohol and a moment of horror when they realised that the person lying next to them was pig ugly/their best mate's man/their man's best mate/a total stranger whose name was a bigger mystery than why men can't grasp the concept of removing their socks before their trousers.

But, even though this book is all about brief encounters, don't go assuming that casual sex is for everyone. While some people can easily handle the false intimacy and regular rejection that goes hand-in-hand with a rampant lifestyle, others are much better off sticking with their right hand until they meet Mr Right. If you can't handle casual sex, it doesn't mean that you're old-fashioned or frigid. Conversely, if you're working your way through the phone book alphabetically, it doesn't make you a slut. Enjoying casual sex is just down to your personality. If it makes you feel happy, great. If not, don't do it. You can have a lot of fun without getting laid.

So, should you be going for brief encounters? In true sex manual style, this checklist will help you establish whether casual sex is for you.

Do you enjoy sex?
It may seem obvious, but a lot of people go for casual sex when actually they want affection, love or diamonds. If you're going to sleep around, it should be an end in itself, rather than a way of getting what you want. Otherwise, you'll end up heartbroken and/or bitter, and that's no fun at all.

Are you comfortable insisting on safer sex, no matter how drunk you are?
If the answer is no, get to a nunnery now. Have you *seen* pictures of sexually transmitted infections? They're a great way to seriously reduce your quality of life; and that's if you get one of the ones that doesn't end your life altogether. Hey, just because this book is about casual sex, it doesn't

mean you'll get away with behaving irresponsibly, except in fun ways. Luckily, sexually transmitted infections are easy to avoid if you're intelligent about it and use a condom. If you're not happy with safer sex, don't sleep around.

If a guy doesn't cuddle you after sex, can you just write it off as 'one of those things'?
Some men cuddle, some don't. If you're in a relationship, it's all very well to expect affection and, if a bloke's polite, he'll probably curl up with you after sex, even if you both know it was a 'one-night-only' thing. But not everyone you have sex with will necessarily be affectionate. Deal with it. You got laid, didn't you? If you can't live without cuddles, get a dog. Sure, it needs walking and feeding, but it's way more likely to give you affection than some random man you've pulled.

Are you (broadly) happy with your body?
Having sex to get reassurance is common enough, and anyone who says they don't get an ego boost from being found sexually attractive is a liar. However, brief encounters don't always lead to compliments, and some rude sods may make personal comments about your body, so you need to have a good sense of perspective about the way you look (which amounts to 'I am gorgeous and anyone who says otherwise is a meanie'). Get your self-esteem from within, not from the people you fuck. Oh, and if someone who's been lucky

enough to get into your knickers insults you, don't put out. He clearly doesn't deserve to have sex with a babe like you.

If a man says he'll call, can you go out rather than sit chained to the phone?

Almost every woman has spent time waiting for the phone to ring. It's soul-destroying and wastes time that could otherwise be spent drinking cocktails. If a man wants to get hold of you, he'll call. If he doesn't call, it's not because he's dead/in a coma/has moved to Outer Mongolia. He just doesn't want to call. It doesn't mean that you were crap in the sack. It just means that he was happy with his lot and doesn't see any need to take things further.

That said, it's worth being aware of the concept of 'boy-time'. A woman will normally be waiting for the phone to ring from the second that she leaves a guy's house. A man won't generally think about calling for at least three days, for fear of being seen as desperate/ over-keen/a loser. To men, a week is well within acceptable time-lag between sex and phone call. If it gets to ten days, he ain't calling. Up to that point, put on the answerphone, enjoy partying and get on with your life. You can be sure as hell that he will be.

Do you want to?

It may sound stupid, but there are some people out there who have casual sex because they feel like they should.

Regardless of what the media or your mates may say, the only person who knows whether you should have sex is you.

Don't have sex because all your mates are obsessed with pulling. Don't have sex because you feel like you need to in order to be a cool urban chick. Don't have sex because some guy you don't really fancy is being terribly persistent. Only have sex if you really want it. And if you want sex, go for it as much as you want.

Sounds OK so far? Great. But there are some things that mean casual sex certainly isn't for you. If any of the below are true, avoid, avoid, avoid. Trust me, you'll be far happier that way.

You're underage
It may seem unfair – then again, everything does at your age – but, honestly, sex is much better if you wait. Really. It's not just a line that the Mothers' Union paid to have included in the book.

Sex isn't just about rubbing body parts together; your head and heart tend to get involved too, and it's much harder to separate those things when you're young; added to which, it's hard to get a second date if your man's been banged up for having sex with a minor. So stick to masturbation; it's way easier and you'll probably get a lot more enjoyment out of it than you will from nervous fumblings with an inept teenage boy, or sex with some older pervert who likes young girls. Plus, by getting to know your own body, you'll be more likely to have fantastic sex when you are old enough.

You don't really enjoy sex and just do it to get attention
Casual sex may get you someone's undivided attention for the time that you're actually doing it but, once a guy's shot his load, the attention rapidly fades. If you only have sex to get attention, it's best avoiding casual action until after you've worked on your confidence. Sex only provides a very quick ego-boost and, long-term, casual sex is more likely to batter your self-esteem than boost it.

You'll get far more positive attention by letting your real personality shine through and liking yourself than you will by getting naked at every opportunity. The reason for having casual sex is because you want sex, not because you want to be loved.

You fall in love with everyone you have sex with
That's dead sweet but, if you sleep around, you may well turn bunny-boiler, and that's just not nice behaviour. You can still get some sex tips from this book, but save them for when you find your perfect partner because life's too short to waste dealing with court orders for harassment, men shrinking back in fear at the mention of your name or simply feeling sad.

Test your 'falling in love' quotient

If you're still on the fence about whether or not casual sex is for you, it's worth checking your 'falling in love' quotient. Heavy emotions and casual sex don't go together. That said, it is possible to be a romantic and still get your rocks off with a gazillion strangers without going mad. You just need to make sure that your clit doesn't double as a 'love-button': when someone presses it, your heart gets involved. (NB: If you're with a bloke and he actually calls your clit a love-button, walk out immediately. He's clearly watched far too much bad porn.)

So, without further ado, on with the quiz:

1. *You see someone you fancy in a bar. Do you:*
   a) Smile at him in such a way as to make his underwear melt and offer him a drink?
   b) Check out his clothes to see how rich he is?
   c) Listen in on his conversation to see whether you have anything in common?
   d) Mentally plan the wedding and name your children?

2. *How long do you wait before putting out?*
   a) Wait? Why bother?
   b) Until he's taken you out to dinner at the most exclusive restaurants in town, bought up all your local flower shop and half of Tiffany's and you need to put out to secure the flash holiday.

c) Three dates — you want him to respect you.

d) Until he's got the ring on your finger.

3. *It's the morning after a heated night. Do you:*

a) Sneak out without waking him, even if it means leaving your undies behind because you can't find them?

b) Ask him when he's taking you to the fabulous and terribly expensive restaurant that you casually mentioned (ten times) last night?

c) Give him your number and wait for the phone to ring, or take his number and call a few days later?

d) Ask him when you're meeting his parents?

4. *He hasn't called you a week after your first encounter. Do you:*

a) Move on to your next target; it saves embarrassment as you're not entirely sure what his name was anyway?

b) Call him and explain, sweetly, that unless he sends you that fabulous diamond bracelet you saw in the window of a terribly expensive boutique, you'll tell his wife/company/the press exactly what he wanted you to do with the piping bag and stick of celery.

c) Give him another three days to call and write him off as a waste of space if he doesn't get back to you by then.

d) Sob into your pillow and call *The Times* to cancel the engagement notice.

If you answered mostly a's, you're perfectly suited to casual sex. You see it as it should be seen: a bit of fun to pass the time and give you orgasms.

If you answered mostly b's, you're in it for the money, not the sex. Fine, if you want to be like that, but if you think of men as wallets then they're perfectly justified in thinking of you as a hooker.

If you answered mostly c's, you're after a boyfriend, not a shag, but you can probably do the casual sex thing as long as you keep your emotions under control.

And if you answered mostly d's, don't even think about having casual sex. You'll get your heart broken endlessly. Which is upsetting, not to mention fattening, as there's only so much ice-cream a girl can eat before her thighs revolt.

The many ages of casual sex

Now you know whether or not brief encounters are for you, it's time to probe a little deeper into the casual sex lifestyle. Taking as read the age of consent, brief encounters can be fun at any age. Common times for it include:

16-18: You've just discovered sex and want to try it as much as possible. Bear in mind that, the younger you are, the more likely it is that you're having sex to boost your self-esteem. This doesn't make you a bad person. It's just worth being aware of because it can be bad for you in the long run. If you need to have sex with someone to make him or her like you, then they're not worth knowing.

Early twenties: Particularly if you're a student. You've got a ready-made social life and access to cheap alcohol and easy blokes. You lucky sod. Take advantage of it while you can; if you cling on to the boyfriend you've had since you were fifteen because you need a security blanket, it's all too likely that he'll dump you on graduation day leaving you pining for all the sex you could have had.

Mid twenties: Maybe you've realised that finding Mr Right is too hard and you'd rather have fun with Mr Right Now until he comes along. Or perhaps you've had a long-term relationship and messy break-up so want to prove you're still sexy, find out what you were missing out on and make your ex jealous of the attention you're getting. (NB: If you're doing it solely for the latter reason, it may not be all that good for you. But if you're sleeping with loads of people because you want to, and your ex dumped you/ran off with someone else, hell, rub his nose in it.)

30+: You may have kids and, if you've been married for any length of time, you're almost certainly unsure of how dating works nowadays because it's been a while since you were on the scene. Don't worry. It hasn't changed that much. The first date is the hardest but once that's out the way, you'll soon realise that men are just as much of a nightmare – and a joy – as they were the last time you were dating.

Don't worry if you don't fall into one of these categories; everyone is different and there are as many reasons for indulging in recreational sex as there are fabulous shoes at Jimmy Choo's. The main thing to remember is that, if you like the idea of casual sex and you can be responsible about it, then it can be a hell of a lot of fun.

Of course, not everyone will appreciate that you want to indulge in sensual sweatiness with strangers. Sexual equality may have come a long way but there's still that glorious double standard of 'man who sleeps around = stud: woman who sleeps around = slut'. Some people will try to make you feel guilty about your choice, and others may question your motives. Sod them! If you're happy – and your partners are – then the rest of the world is irrelevant.

If you're really concerned about what people think, just don't tell them. It's not as if they've got a webcam in your bedroom. (If they have, then they're in no position to question your morals.) But just in case you want some ammunition to debunk their spurious comments, here's some myth-busting material:

Common myths about brief encounters

Women only have casual sex because they've got self-esteem issues
This harks back to the days when women were expected to be happy looking after their man and getting housekeeping in exchange for doing all the cooking and cleaning, and is just as outdated. While casual sex is sometimes used as a confidence-booster, for men as well as women, it's by no means always the case.

Shockingly enough, women like sex just as much as men do; and they're just as capable of having no-strings sex as men are. The difference is that women are conditioned to think that sleeping around is something to be ashamed of, whereas men grow up perceiving it as 'stud-like' behaviour. Shagging because you fancy a shag isn't seen as acceptable for women, just as working was seen as unacceptable for women 30 or so years ago. So if you're sleeping around and feeling good on it, ignore the people touting around this myth. They're just being sexist.

There are warning signs to look out for, though. If you only feel happy when you're flirting or being flirted with, then your self-esteem may be too heavily tied to your sexuality. If you feel great when you pull, but lousy after – or even during – sex, then there could be something deeper at work, and it's worth taking time out and maybe seeking counselling. A period of celibacy is something that every woman should try for a while anyway; it's a great way of figuring out who you really are and what you really want. And, my God, will you enjoy the first fuck you have afterwards.

If you sleep with a man too soon, he won't respect you
'Will you still respect me in the morning?'
    'I don't respect you now.'
    Never a truer line has been said. It takes more than a bit of spit-swapping to make someone lose respect. If a man

doesn't respect you after a night of hot action, he didn't respect you to start with. Sure, there are blokes out there with the virgin/whore syndrome embedded firmly in their psyche, but one shag from a man like that is quite enough anyway (even one shag can be bad enough).

More to the point, respect from other people is way less important than self-respect. Ask not 'Will he respect me in the morning' but 'Will I respect myself?'

If you sleep with too many people, you'll never find true love
Worried that you'll put off Mr Right by sleeping with a load of people before you find him? Fret no more. If he's right for you, he won't care. Having a variety of brief encounters means that by the time you do find that perfect person, you'll be more aware of what you like and dislike in bed, you'll have learned about the infinite quirks of men and you may have a hot tale of lesbo lust that you can tell Mr Right about in graphic detail when his ardour starts to droop.

Getting some experience before you settle down also means that you can enter into a long-term relationship without any 'What if … ?' thoughts, which can make it easier to have a successful relationship. Just remember, if you do get hitched, no matter how many guys you've had, the one that you settle down with is the best lover ever – even (particularly!) if he isn't.

Women who sleep around will get into trouble
Sleeping with lots of people won't necessarily lead to sexually transmitted infections, pregnancy or being a 'fallen woman'. As long as you behave responsibly – use condoms, ideally teamed with some other form of contraception, be aware of the risks and act accordingly – then you can have fun without having a life of shame.

Life as an uber-vixen

So, you've decided that casual sex is for you. What can you expect by embracing the lifestyle? Well, it may seem rather screamingly obvious but, err, more sex. According to the Durex Report, the average Brit has sex 119 times a year whereas the average American is getting it 111 times a year. The British Sexual Survey reports that married women aged 16–24 get it six times a month, dropping to a mere twice a month by the time they get to 45. So, single girls are getting nearly double the sex of their married counterparts. Remember that the next time an attached mate gets smug on you.

Casual sex is a great way to learn new tricks, too. No two people are the same in the sack; they all have different erogenous zones, kinks and techniques. Make a point of paying attention because that way, should you ever decide to settle down, you'll be a truly sensational lover. Of course, it's probably a good idea to tell your eventual man that you learned all your sex tricks from a book rather than getting laid by the planet, because otherwise it might distress the delicate little flower, but men can be gullible so that's no biggie.

By indulging in brief encounters, there's also a pretty good chance that you'll make some friends. Yep, you can remain friends with people you've had casual sex with and, unlike staying friends with 'proper' exes, it can be fun and painless. Not to mention that staying mates with your conquests means that you've got access to all their mates too and, with any luck (and a bit of practice), can rely on them to give you a rave review. Be warned, though; you may have the occasional moment of embarrassment when you realise you've shagged 50 per cent of the people you've invited to your birthday party and spend the entire event trying to keep them from swapping amusing stories about you (or considering the various group sex permutations you could go with).

Of course, shagging around isn't all orgasms and thrills. Like anything fun, there are also down-sides. The more partners you have, the higher your risk of contracting a sexually transmitted infection (STI), though the tips in this book will help minimise that risk. You may hear rumours that if someone moans when they go down on you there's an echo (though regular sex can actually help tighten your vag). Unattractive guys may assume that, because you sleep with a fair few people, it means you'll sleep with them. Women may refuse to let you stand near their boyfriends in case you're unable to hold back your wanton self and start copulating with their bloke right there, right then. (NB: women with ugly or otherwise unappealing boyfriends are particularly prone to this.) But look on the bright side. You get to have more sex. And that's what brief encounters are all about.

Essential guidelines for casual sex queens

1. Carry condoms and use them. Always.
2. Banish the words 'I love you' from your vocabulary until you decide that you want to move on from casual sex.
3. Don't expect men to call back. They may well do but, if they don't, it's because they just wanted a one-night stand, not because there's anything wrong with you.
4. Be careful who you talk to about your sex life. It's easy to be branded as a slapper, and even your best mates will get bored if your sole topic of conversation is what you got up to in the sack last night.
5. Keep in mind the 'mates before meat' rule. Seeing your friends is always more important than getting laid (unless you're really horny, obviously).

Chapter 2

The Greatest Love of All

You may be raring for some hot and heavy action but, before you let anyone else into your knickers, you need to know what's going on inside them yourself. After all, if you don't know how to give yourself a blissful night, how can you expect anyone else to? And, more to the point, at the risk of sounding all 'hippy psycho-babble', the most important relationship a woman can have is with herself.

So how do you make sure you love yourself? Don't worry, you're not going to have to stand looking in the mirror making positive affirmations or anything. You just need to masturbate.

'Whipping up the fanny batter' and other charming expressions

'Oi!' you may be saying. 'This is a book about shagging around. What's masturbation got to do with it?' Well, quite a lot. After all, you don't just want to get laid; you want to get laid *well*. If you wanted mediocre sex, then you wouldn't need a book to get it; you'd just need enough money to get a guy hammered. There's no point getting off with people if you don't know what gets you off first. And indulging in self-pleasure is by far the best way to find out what really works for you.

Even better, regular masturbation will increase your pulling chances because it makes you look more gorgeous. Forget the Botox; orgasm gets rid of the tension that restricts blood vessels in the brain, preventing frown lines from deepening. And when you masturbate, you release a hormone called DHEA (dehydroepiandrosterone, to give it it's full name), which gives you glowing skin and acts as an antidepressant so you'll smile more.

Of course, even the most successful trollop has off nights. Masturbation means that when you're home alone, you can still get off. It's free, you don't need any specialist equipment (although toys can be fun – but more of that later) and it provides a useful way of killing time during ad breaks.

Pleasure aside, another great thing about masturbation is that it's *actually good for you*. Orgasm keeps your bones and muscles healthy, lowers stress and generally chills you out. It helps fight off colds and flu by increasing testosterone and oestrogen levels, which boosts your immune system. And it also releases painkilling endorphins and oxytocin – thought to relieve period pain – into your bloodstream. Which, let's face it, is much more fun than taking a load of painkillers and lying down, groaning, with a hot-water bottle on your stomach.

There's no need to feel embarrassed about masturbation; a cliterati.co.uk poll found that the average woman gets it on with herself two to five times per week, and only three per cent of women claim that they never masturbate. Sex toy sales are at an all time high and female masturbation is even mentioned on TV nowadays, so you're just doing what's normal and publicly accepted (as long as you don't do it in public. Or if you do, you make sure you're damned discreet about it).

So, now you've got the science behind it, you can throw aside any guilt.

How orgasm works

You might think that by the time most women reach adulthood, they've got masturbation pretty much down to a fine art but 40 per cent of women have problems achieving orgasm. There can be medical reasons for this, and, if you're worried, get to the doctors. There's no need to be embarrassed because doctors have seen almost everything before.

Sometimes, your mind will put the brakes on during sex so, if you're having a hard time getting off, it's also worth exploring psychological issues. You may want to see a counsellor, or it could be that you can figure out where the problem lies yourself, if you think about what's been going on in your life.

When your mind says yes but your body says no: Rosie's story

One year I found myself at a festival, having just started recovering from a painful break-up with a boyfriend, and started to feel desperately horny. A friend and I initiated a 'hug competition'; going round to all the boys we fancied and asking them to hug each of us in turn and then giving them a rating.

When I got to Adam, a boy I had ogled from afar the previous year, he took me in his arms, holding me tightly and softly started to stroke my back all over. My pussy started to tingle with excitement (yes, it was *that* good!) and then started to throb as I felt the gentle pressure of his cock nudging against me. When the hug finally came to the end I was blushing and it was pretty obvious who my winner was going to be. Somehow he managed to avoid giving my friend a hug but soon a whole group of us ended up sitting down together. I shared an armchair with him and he started stroking my back again and I was tingling again and we were talking and ... without even thinking our lips melted together and our tongues teased and explored.

After two months of singledom the elegance of this kiss was pure ecstasy. We spent the evening and the whole of the next day in each other's pockets, holding hands, kissing whenever we had the opportunity, but when we reached the tent … it just wasn't happening. I was loving the kisses but the second he put his hand into my knickers I knew I couldn't do it. The more he rubbed, the drier my pussy seemed to become, as if it was saying 'Well, I don't know what you're trying to do, honey, but I'm as sure as hell not having him in here'.

In the end I said I just wasn't ready to sleep with anyone yet after the break-up with my previous boyfriend and as the words came out of my mouth I realised it was true. From the outset of Adam and I fooling around I had made it clear that it was just a weekend thing, just some casual festival fun. I was fully intending to have rampant sex with him but the body has a way of telling you when you aren't emotionally ready for something and even though my head thought I was over my ex, my pussy was quite aware that I wasn't!

Adam was very sweet about it all and we carried on hugging and kissing the next day but before long I drifted away from him, after realising he was thinking that we could carry it on after the festival, something I didn't want. Pulling him had made me realise the freedom of being single and I wanted more loving from more people; even if I wasn't ready for sex, there were still a lot of lips I wanted to kiss.

Whether your orgasmic difficulties are down to physical or mental issues, a night of solo passion is one of the most common courses of treatment ('Take two AA batteries and call me in the morning'), so try devoting some time to self-love. If you can't please yourself, then whoever you pull will have no chance.

At the risk of sounding patronising, it's worth quickly covering how female orgasms work. Almost every woman's been in that situation where they really want to come but nothing seems to be doing the trick. Obviously, bodies being awkward things, the more you think 'I must come', the less likely it is to happen. Don't panic. It's just about working your way through the four stages of female sexual response (sounds sexy, doesn't it?). These are:

1. *Arousal/excitement*
Your nipples and clit swell. You get that flippy feeling in your stomach and suddenly having an orgasm becomes more important than shoes and chocolate put together. If you're alone, you'll often find this feeling comes on when you've got a really boring/important chore to do and need some displacement activity; or when that Elton John video of Robert Downey Jnr looking moody in a tight grey T-shirt comes on. Or maybe that's just me.

When you're aroused, all other things can fade into insignificance; that the man concerned is your boss/best mate's dad/a total idiot or that you're in the photocopier room/at your parents' house/in the middle of a press conference with the world's media avidly watching. Remember, there are loads of chemicals flooding through your body when you're feeling horny. Arousal releases chemicals similar to taking an ecstasy tablet, so treat anything that happens when you're under the influence of the horn with care. It's not fate; it's just oxytocin.

2. *Plateau*

Your pulse rate and breathing speed up and your skin flushes. You're horny enough that you can probably hold back a giggle when your partner asks you whether you're his slut now, or begs you to lick it like a lollipop. Well, maybe.

This is the point at which, if a guy stops doing whatever he's doing that's lighting your fire, you're likely to go ballistic unless he puts his hand/tongue/whatever back exactly where it was 30 seconds ago. Most men seem unaware that if something's working, they should carry on doing it. Tell him before you get to the plateau stage so that the poor guy doesn't face plateau-induced wrath.

3. *Orgasm*

The fun bit. Rhythmic pulsing through your bits (every 0.8 seconds, if you want to get scientific about it), clawing at the bed, flaring nostrils, arching feet, dripping sweat, heavy breathing and all that stuff. Though for some reason, having an orgasm tends to involve much more moaning and groaning when you're with a partner than when you're alone, suggesting that some women exaggerate orgasms, as well as faking them. (NB: Faking it is a bad thing to do, so just don't bother. Why encourage a bloke who's not hitting the right spots? You'll only send him out into the world to give more women crap shags, while believing he's an incredible lover.)

The average orgasm lasts ten seconds, although it might seem like an eternity (if you're lucky). This equates to 12 minutes of shagging-induced orgasm per year for the average attached woman and 21 minutes for the average single girl assuming an orgasm with every lay, which is a big assumption to make. Masturbation-made orgasms add between 17 and 43 minutes to your total, depending on whether you're a twice or five-times a week girl. Puts it in perspective, doesn't it; sex being such a major drive for just over an hour a year, at most, of orgasm.

As well as getting your rocks off, you may find that you get all inspired when you're coming, as orgasm sends a surge of activity through the right side of the brain, which is responsible for creativity. Then again, you might be so busy writhing that everything else in your mind becomes irrelevant, even your neighbours banging on the walls.

4. *Resolution*

Your body calms down again and, if anyone touches your clit, you're more than likely to leap off the bed in agony because it's too sensitive. If you're masturbating you'll possibly feel embarrassed at the sordid fantasies that were running through your mind ten seconds ago and, if you're getting laid, the person next to you may seem much less attractive than they were seven minutes ago (the average length of a shag).

Mind-blowing masturbation

So now you know how it all works, your mission, should you choose to accept it, is to spend time masturbating and figure out what it is that gets you to that plateau — and beyond.

As the song so rightly says, there are three steps to heaven: in this case, mind, body and bits. Spend time on all three and your orgasm awaits. Once you've got to grips with your body, you can share the joy with every man you meet. Well, the fit ones anyway.

Step one: get your mind in gear

When it comes to, err, coming, the first essential is relaxation. Some people can relax easily but if you're more wound up than a complicated bondage knot, set the mood by putting on some sexy music. Have a bath with essential oils like sandalwood or ylang ylang, renowned for their aphrodisiac qualities. Make sure you've got the house to yourself or are in a room with a lockable door where you won't be disturbed. Nothing kills the mood like your mum or flatmate bursting in while you're at it (unless your flatmate is particularly cute). You may want to have a glass of wine to help you get in the mood, but don't have too much, as alcohol can make it harder to come.

Now start thinking horny thoughts. The most important sex organ in the body is the brain, so making sure that it's properly stimulated is a good way to boost your orgasmic chances. You may want to remember a hot night you've had, think of a particular person or just let your imagination wander free. If you're short on inspiration, get a helping hand from Black Lace books or erotic story websites like cliterati.co.uk (run by the author – please excuse the shameless plug).

Some women like looking at visual porn, and there are loads more female-friendly sex shops and websites nowadays so you can find a decent video without having to brave the dirty mac brigade in some seedy sex shop. Oh, and ignore what you've heard about men liking pictures and women liking words. Actually, women get just as physically aroused by visual stuff as men, so don't feel guilty if you've got a selection of films that would make a soldier blush.

If you like the idea of pervy pics but think that the men in the average porn film are hideous, you may want to consider gay porn. Those boys are foxy, and a third of women get off on seeing guys get it on, so you could open up a whole new world of fantasy …

Step two: warming up

Regardless of the method you use to get your juices flowing, once you're there, it's time to get physical because, surprisingly enough, being touched in the right place, in the right way will help you have an orgasm.

Don't just go straight for your clit. You'd think a man was crap if he did, so why do it when you're alone? Instead, try stroking your neck, breasts and anywhere else you enjoy being touched.

The skin is the largest erogenous zone, so maybe start by rubbing body lotion into every inch of your body (except your pink bits: you don't want to encourage thrush). Many women like rubbing or pinching their nipples. If you're one, you may find a set of nipple clamps helps you multi-task. They sound scary but you can get clamps that apply very mild pressure nowadays, so don't think you have to be a pain-queen to enjoy them. (Though if you are a pain-queen, clothes pegs make a cheap do-it-yourself alternative.)

As you get more aroused, move your hands (but not the clamps unless you're very pain driven) lower down. Many women find stimulating the pubic mound (the bit your pubes cover, assuming you don't have a shaven haven) arousing. And pressing on the ovaries – equidistant between your navel and waist – can also hit the spot for some women. Be aware that they may be over-sensitive during ovulation. Give yourself a thorough stroking anywhere and everywhere you like being touched. If you're not sure where that is, now's the time to find out.

Once you're feeling all tingly, start getting more intimate with yourself; but, before you head south, get out the lube. It's a great addition to any sexual act, including masturbation. NB: Never use anything that hasn't been designed as a lubricant on your bits – other oils can rot condoms or encourage thrush.

Step three: clit and the bits (not a sixties girl group)

Now you're lust-crazed and lubed up, you can get onto the meat of the matter and start caressing your clit and labia. Vary the way that you touch yourself to see which you most enjoy, for example:

- Stroking the hood of the clit.
- Putting one finger on either side of your clit and masturbating it like a miniature penis.
- Moving your finger rapidly from side to side over your clit.
- Circling your finger around the tip of your clit.
- Pushing the clitoral hood gently back and stroking the tip of your clit.
- Stroking around your labia majora (outer lips) and/or labia minora (inner lips), both of which are densely packed with nerve endings.
- Rubbing your labia majora together.

- Gently tugging your pubes upwards to move your clitoral hood up and down over your clitoris.
- Gently pinching your labia majora and/or clitoris.
- Tapping your clit with one finger.
- Gently slapping your pubic mound and/or labia.
- Stretching open your labia majora with one hand and stroking your clit and/or labia minora with the other hand.

You may want to slide your fingers inside yourself but don't feel obliged. Only 25 per cent of women climax through penetration alone and most women can achieve orgasm far more easily through clitoral stimulation. That said, it's worth experimenting with different techniques, so you may want to give one of these finger-penetration variations a go:

- Sliding one or more fingers in and out slowly.
- Alternating two fingers piston-style.
- Slipping a finger or more inside you and flexing your Kegel (pelvic floor) muscles around it.
- Moving one or more fingers inside yourself in a circular motion.
- Holding your wrist with one hand and using it to push a finger or fingers of the other hand inside yourself.
- Putting just the tip of your finger inside yourself and moving it rapidly in and out.
- Self-fisting (see box).

Self-fisting: less scary than it sounds

If you're into penetration then you might want to try vaginal fisting. Despite the word being as intimidating as hell, it can be an intense way to orgasm. It's far easier with a partner unless you have very bendy wrists but, if you want to test out whether it's for you, try it first with the person you can trust the most; yourself.

To start with, cut your nails and make sure you don't have any rough bits of skin that could scratch your bits. You may want to use a latex glove to make it more comfortable (and should definitely make your partner wear a glove if you're being fisted by them, to protect against STIs). Remove any jewellery – including your watch – and cover your hand in a lot of lube. Then add more lube. Then add some more. One more squirt of lube after that and you're ready, but keep the lube nearby for regular top-ups.

Despite what the name suggests, you don't start with your hand in a fist. It's actually a gentle activity if it's done properly. Put first one finger, then two inside you and only add more as you get more aroused. It's not a race and, if it's not giving you the horn, you don't need to carry on.

Assuming that you do like it, when you're easily taking four fingers, pull your hand out and squish your fingers together into a shadow-puppet rabbit shape (but without the ears!) Slide your hand gently inside yourself, twisting it from side to side to help ease it in. Stop every so often so that your vagina gets used to being stretched and, if it hurts, pull your hand slowly out.

Once you get to the knuckles, twist your hand more to get it inside you. The angle is pretty tricky, so you may need to use your other hand to help ease your fist inside yourself. Adding some extra stimulation with a vibrator on your clit can make it easier to take your whole hand. Similarly, tensing then releasing your Kegel muscles can help your vagina suck in your hand.

Once your hand is inside you, it's way easier to relax, because the neck of your vagina is stretched around your wrist, which is only as thick as a really large cock, rather than your fist, which is considerably bigger. You'll be surprised at how large your vagina is; it easily stretches to accommodate a fist.

Chances are, your fingers will naturally curl under to form a fist. If you're really flexible, there's a slim chance you can reach your G-spot but, if not, you'll still be stimulating your clitoris indirectly by stretching the skin of the clitoral hood tightly over it.

Slide your hand up and down – without withdrawing your knuckles – for as long as you want, then, when you've had enough, slowly twist your hand out of your vagina. You may have already climaxed but, if not, finish the job with your favourite form of stimulation. Or just go and do the washing up/get back to work; it's entirely up to you. (Wash your hands first though; you don't want things getting messy.)

NB: Fisting can damage nerves in the bladder, G-spot, urethral sphincter and cervix through abrasion or over-stretching. It can also encourage cystitis so, if you're going to give it a go, wash your hands first, remember the lube and take it very slowly and gently.

Alternatively, go for one of numerous toys out there. They can provide fun in ways that your fingers can't, and can take a lot less effort, so are ideal for when you're feeling lazy (or drunk).

Anal action

The anus: for some women an area of joy and pleasure, for others, the part of their body that unpleasant stuff comes out of and for yet others, the reason they learn how to punch, as they deal with men using the 'sorry, wrong hole' line.

If you fall into the first category, then don't neglect your backside when you're indulging in self-pleasure. Just make sure that you're prepared for it first. It's even more important than with vaginal and clitoral masturbation that you wash your hands and trim those fingernails back before you go shoving a finger when the sun doesn't shine; the anus has much thinner skin than the vagina so is more vulnerable to tears. And, unlike the vagina, it doesn't lubricate itself, so you absolutely have to use lube. It should go without saying, but please make sure you wash your hands afterwards, so you don't get food poisoning. A latex glove can be a useful addition to anal masturbation, too, particularly if you don't want to mess up your manicure.

Some ways of getting anal thrills include:

- Running a lubricated finger around the outer sphincter (rim) of your anus.
- Rubbing the side of your hand between your cheeks and over your anus (careful not to rub your vagina with that hand though – you don't want to encourage cystitis or thrush).
- Sliding one or more fingers gently inside your anus.
- Going for a double whammy with one finger in your anus and the other in your vagina ...

- … or hitting the treble with a finger in both anus and vagina, and fingers from the other hand stroking your clit.
- Gently pistoning two fingers in and out of your anus.
- Using one hand to gently stretch yourself open while the other teases the inner sphincter of the anus.

NB: As with your vagina and clit, there are loads of toys designed to pleasure your arse. But make sure that you don't move anything that's touched your anus into your vagina or onto your clit afterwards (or during), otherwise you're heading for thrush and other infections that can put your bits out of action.

Other masturbation tricks

Once you've experimented with all the various bodily parts that can give you pleasure, think about moving onto some more creative self-loving techniques.

- Rub yourself through the seam of your jeans, with your fingers or the spine of a book.
- Grind against a pillow.
- Pull the crotch of your knickers up and rub against it.
- Rub your thighs together.
- Hump the arm of the sofa.
- Flex your Kegel muscles to see if you can make yourself come without touching yourself at all. If you can, it certainly spices up public transport.

You can also focus on learning more about your body to help you direct a partner when you've got them into the sack:

- Try holding yourself back the first time you approach orgasm to see if that makes your eventual orgasm better.
- Take yourself to the edge, then pull back, to see if you can identify exactly what it is that triggers your orgasm.
- See how many orgasms you like to have in a row.
- Make a mental note of where and how you touch yourself to take you over the edge quickly.
- Figure out what you do if you want more of a 'slow-burn' experience.
- Spend an afternoon testing which smells, tastes and textures get you off.

The more you know about yourself, the more sexual confidence you'll have and the better sex you'll get. It doesn't matter what you try, as long as it's safe; just stop if you don't like it and, if you love it, add it to your repertoire.

Sex toys

A 'finger of fun' may be just enough but why settle for 'enough' when sex toys can add so much more to the equation? We've come a long way since the days of a hard dildo being the only option. Now, you can get toys in all shapes and sizes.

When it comes to anything that you put in intimate places, it's best to play it safe. Certain plastic vibrators

Things never to use for masturbation

- Any fruit or veg that hasn't been thoroughly washed or peeled. They can have nasty pesticides on the outside of them, and bananas have a tendency to split. (Surely I don't need to tell you not to let citrus fruit near your bits?)
- Coloured candles: the dye can come off (try explaining that one when you pull).
- Deodorant bottles: the cap can come off leading to an embarrassing trip to casualty.
- Anyone else's electric toothbrush: what kind of a slapper are you to even consider it? If you're using your own electric toothbrush, make sure the bristles are well covered in several layers of freezer-bag first.

NB: This is by no means an exhaustive list, so, as a golden rule, if in doubt, don't.

have levels of CFCs that have been linked to cervical cancer. With this in mind, you may want to go for silicone, crystal or even wood instead of rubber. Sex toy specialists, Mantric, put it concisely: 'If your toy smells like a shower curtain when you open the box, don't use it without a condom; it's probably got the nasty plastics that have been linked to cancers in it.'

As a rough guide, toys fall into two main categories: dildos and vibrators. Dildos don't vibrate and are generally phallic in shape. They can be used on their own for that full-up feeling, or with a harness for strap-on fun (always a good way to get a bloke to stop hassling you for anal sex – just use the 'I will if you do first' line).

If you get a dildo with a suction cup, it can be stuck to a wall (of the shower, if you like the whole spray over your clit sensation) so you can buck back against it. (NB: This is probably one of the most embarrassing ways to be caught using a toy so make extra-sure that the door is locked.)

And then there are vibrators, which, shockingly enough, vibrate. To make your vibe last longer, take the batteries out after use. You don't want the embarrassment of getting your toy out to use in front of a guy and it buzzing once then stopping. Female masturbation is cool and something that gives blokes the horn, but they probably don't want to think that your entire life is devoted to it.

Vibrators come in numerous shapes and sizes, from your standard cock substitutes to the glorious 'more than just a cock' Jessica Rabbit-style toys, which combine a clitoral stimulator with a rotating shaft. There's also been a trend in recent years for non-phallic toys, from the quirky, like the Rubber Duckie (a rubber duck-shaped toy, which is also waterproof) to the 'ergonomic' (Candida Royale's 'Natural Contours' range) that look more like designer phones than sex toys.

Wireless toys are another hot new trend; they can be remote controlled using a special key-ring from up to 500 feet away and add a pervy chat-up line to any woman's pulling arsenal; 'Can you look after the controls for my sex toy?' This has the added bonus of leaving a man in no doubt as to what you're after – but don't try it unless you trust him; men like gadgets so he might not be able to stop pressing your button.

And then there are toys for anal action. From the small and sweet vibes to big and brazen butt-plugs, the golden rule of toys for the back passage is never put in anything that you can't get out. In practice, this means ensuring that the toy has a flared base or a 'string' so that it's easy to remove; you so don't want *that* trip to casualty.

Men tend to be less intimidated by non-phallic or small toys, but your sex toy choice should be about what you want, not what your casual shag wants. Just keep the 12-inch maxi-vibra-dong safely in a cupboard when you go out on the pull, so that the poor lad you drag home with you doesn't suffer performance anxiety.

Using your toy

Most women tend to use vibrators to stimulate their clit but, as with any other form of masturbation, getting creative can deliver fantastic results. Try running a vibrator over your pubic mound, or use it to stimulate just the hood of your clit. Alternatively, push back your clitoral hood and use a vibe on the lowest setting to tease the tip of it. Handle with care though, because the clitoral tip is incredibly sensitive and you want to be moaning with pleasure, not yelping with pain.

Take a dildo or waterproof vibrator into the shower with you, and use it in combination with the shower spray for double thrills. Or slide a toy inside yourself and see if you can climax just by flexing your muscles around it.

The fabulous Sadie Allison, author of *Tickle Your Fancy: A Woman's Guide to Sexual Self Pleasure* has a good trick to make masturbating feel more like shagging:

'Straddling a dildo is a great thing to explore. Stack several pillows into a mound ... Lay a towel over the pillows before straddling the mound. Place the dildo underneath yourself and let it glide up inside you.'

Get experimental with your toy; after all, no-one else can see what you're doing so it's the perfect time to see what you really want. And once you've got it down to a fine art, you're ready for a real 'sex-goddess' technique; putting on a toy show for the guy you've pulled (see Chapter 5). Toys may be designed with solo pleasure in mind, but they'll add an extra frisson to sexual encounters and help you mark your place in a partner's mind as their ultimate lover.

Masturbation resources

There are myriad ways in which you can enjoy masturbation. The following resources provide education, inspiration or stimulation, which has got to be a good thing.

Sex for One: The Joy of Selfloving by Betty Dodson
A classic text containing masturbation tips and informative line drawings to help you find your way around your body.

My Secret Garden by Nancy Friday
Contains hundreds of women's sexual fantasies to give you pervy inspiration.

Earotica CD (For more info see richsensations.com)
A range of erotic CDs designed for women, featuring sexy men reading sensual stories. All CDs come with free rose quartz and incense to help set the mood.

Vielle (For more info, see vielle.info)
Reduces the amount of time it takes women to climax from 13 minutes to just under six minutes, according to clinical trials.

Now you know how to pleasure yourself, it's time to move on to getting pleasured by someone else. After all, that's what being free and single is all about. But what kind of brief encounter should you go for? Casual sex isn't just about one-night-stands; it can cover a range of pleasures from sex with an ex to hiring an escort, enjoying a fuck-buddy to having femme-on-femme fun or even just enjoying some mutual masturbation online. The choice is yours.

Chapter 3

Casual Relationship Types

So, you've established that you're emotionally able to enjoy brief encounters. You're positively glistening with excitement at the prospect of throwing caution (and your knickers) aside and entering into a life of carnal pleasure.

But stop.

There's more to this casual sex thing than just going up to some bloke, saying 'Fancy a fuck?' and taking him back to your place for a night of hot and sordid action. OK, not much, but there are a fair few ways to enjoy being young, free and single, so it's worth considering all the options to figure out which is best for you.

Some women are into the 'Wham, bam, thank you man' appeal of one-night stands, while others prefer a more exclusive 'fuck-buddy' approach. Some find that sex with an ex is the easiest way to scratch their itch and a rare — rich — few prefer to pay for their passion.

And brief encounters don't always involve pulling men. Over a third of women are bi-curious, so knowing how best to get a woman into bed without ruining any friendship that you may have can be a useful skill to have.

Which one's for you? Only you can tell. But the following pointers should help you figure it out.

Stay Safe

If you go on the pull or out on a date with someone new, tell a friend where you're going and what time you'll be back, arrange for someone to call to check you're OK an hour or so into the date, arrange your own transport home and don't go anywhere unfamiliar that you couldn't get away from at speed. Keeping yourself safe is essential.

One night in heaven: your guide to one-night stands

Mention casual sex and most people will automatically think of one-night stands. They're the fast-food of the sex world; relatively easy to get — for women, at least — and can satisfy a craving quickly and easily.

That said, they're not entirely ideal. While it's entirely possible to have good sex on a one-night stand, a lot of men see it as little more than a 'de-spunking' and pay very little attention to what you want. One-night stands are also the easiest way to get a bad reputation. No matter how unfair it is, if you go to your local nightclub and realise you already know what every guy there is like in the sack, chances are there will be some graffiti in the toilets dedicated to you.

How to get a one-night stand

Be brazen. This is no time to be a shrinking violet (whatever that is). Approach your target and make your intentions clear. If you're in a club, this can be by gyrating against him when you dance. If you're in a pub, you could offer to buy him a drink. Now that there are dangers like drink-spiking out there, it's best to be careful if he offers to return the favour though. Watch to make sure that he doesn't slip anything into it – ecstasy, date-rape drug Rohypnol or whatever. You want to be conscious (and aware of the person you're getting it on with) when you do get him home.

Where to go

If you're feeling extravagant, by far the best place to take your one-night stand is a hotel. If he turns scary, there's hotel security. If you've lied about your name or lifestyle, there are no clues lurking around the place to trip you up. And no matter how messy things get, you don't have to clear up afterwards.

If your income level is more 'pint of water' than 'bottle of champagne', you're left with two choices (unless he's prepared to stump for a hotel): your place or his. If you go for a 'home game', you won't have to navigate your way back from an unfamiliar area the next morning, you've got easy access to your make-up and clothes and you can rest safe in the knowledge that the only kinky sex toys around the place are ones that you've bought. However, it does mean that he knows where you live; and the onus is on you to kick him out.

If you go back to his place, you get to maintain an air of mystery, which is far harder when you have to move a pile of washing off the bed before he can sit down. However, you run the risk of encountering an array of bondage equipment or, even scarier, a room that smells of stinky socks and walls full of topless girls beaming down at you. That said, you can make your excuses and leave if his place is really repellent, and he'll have no idea how to find you.

Of course, if you're really desperate, you could just fuck your conquest in a back alley and then make your own way home, but it doesn't really lend itself to hours of exquisite foreplay.

What to do

Ignoring the obvious, one-night stands are a great way to test out different sides of your character and explore new kinks – up to a point. Power games have no place in one-night stands because they require trust and, no matter how nice someone seems, you don't want a virtual stranger to have you handcuffed. But other than that, do whatever you want – as always, with a condom.

After you've had your fun, you can either go home or stay curled up with him. Make your excuses and leave in the morning, though; it's got far more dignity than trying to inveigle a date out of him. You can always leave your number and, if he likes you, he'll call. If he doesn't call, he hasn't died, left the country or realised that he's secretly gay. He's just enjoyed the encounter for what it was. See it in the same way and you'll keep your self-esteem in one piece.

Pros
- If it's rubbish, you don't have to do it again.
- It's pretty easy to keep an emotional distance.
- You can live out your fantasies without having to commit yourself to a lifestyle.

Cons
- If it's good, you don't get to do it again.
- More partners = more risk of STIs.

- You run out of potential conquests quicker.
- Can be a bit soulless.

One perfect night: Mia's story

I met Chris at a corporate party I'd organised. He asked me if I wanted to dance early on in the evening, but I was too busy doing the hostess thing to say yes. When he came back later in the evening, I knew that he was keen and I'd finished working by then, so I accepted his offer of a drink. One drink became several and I ended up swapping tops with him on the dance-floor; something that particularly impressed him because I wasn't wearing a bra.

He invited me back to his place but I declined, because I was shattered, instead agreeing to meet him that weekend. I wasn't looking for anything serious, but from what I'd seen of his body, I was looking forward to exploring things further.

The weekend came, and it soon became obvious that we both had the same thing in mind; within 20 minutes, we both admitted it. He was as much of a tease as me though, so we ended up having drinks, dinner and several games of pool before heading back to his place.

As soon as we got into the taxi, our hands were all over each other; just feeling his hand on my thigh was enough to make me want more. We realised that, despite agreeing we'd have sex, we had no idea how compatible we were, so had a snog. It was intense, and we practically ran out of the cab to his flat.

When we got inside, I was impressed to see that it was clean and stylish; but I wasn't there for home décor. He led me into his room, with its velvet duvet, pushed me to the bed, pinning my arms over my head, and we started kissing in earnest. Things rapidly progressed and by six o'clock the following morning, he'd had eight orgasms and I'd lost count of the amount that I'd had.

We had a coffee together and he drove me to the station in his sports car. Even though we'd agreed to do it again, it didn't come as a surprise when he never called. We'd both had a fantastic time, but it was too good for me to want to ruin the memory by chasing him.

Just one night? Amanda's story

I had a one-night stand with an unusual twist. I'd been out clubbing one Friday with my friends in the city when I clocked this incredibly hot guy of about 29. After I smiled at him, he came over and chatted me up. We did some 'dirty dancing' and, after clearing it with my flat mate, I asked James back to our flat.

I didn't really have one-nighters but I'd been without a boyfriend for months and was, quite frankly, horny. I decided that if I was going to sleep with someone I'd pulled at a club, I may as well get what I wanted out of it; loads of pleasure. So, unlike my usual way in bed, which can only be described as 'good old-fashioned girly' where the man does the initiating, I was quite demanding of James. He in turn seemed to get off on being with a sexually confident woman. Let's just say by morning we were both exhausted.

He'd set his mobile alarm, telling me he had an early appointment, even though it was Saturday. I didn't ask but I suspected he was one of these guys who didn't want to make small talk in the morning. It was fine with me anyway as I was looking for a new flat that day.

Later that morning, as I pulled up outside the flat I was viewing, I was surprised to see James there, just as he was surprised to see me! It turned out that he was the letting agent showing the flat I was interested in seeing.

Not only did I agree to take the flat, I also I took James in it. The moral of this story is: if you're going to have a one-night stand get what you want out of it (ie great sex!) or what's the point?'

More than 'just good friends': the fuck-buddy lifestyle

One of the more recent trends is that of the 'fuck-buddy', or 'sex-friend', falling somewhere between a full-on relationship and a one-night stand. Fuck-buddies can be a handy addition to the casual lifestyle, as they're generally around to provide a helping hand – or whatever – when you need it most.

The most successful fuck-buddy relationships are those in which the 'buddy' is as important as the 'fuck'. Sex isn't just about satisfying a physical urge, and a good fuck-buddy will understand this, giving you affection without attachment, and lust without love. But remember, it goes both ways; if you expect to be able to pick up the phone and get a man delivered hot and ready to your door, you've got to be prepared to satisfy his hunger on demand too.

Make sure that you're clear about the nature of your relationship from day one. It's not fair to lead a guy on if you're only offering passion and he wants commitment. Give him the chance to opt out before he's sampled your skills in the sack; what hope does the poor sucker have of saying no afterwards? With the right handling, a fuck-buddy can sustain a woman for a fair few nights. Just be wary not to let it turn into a relationship, unless that's what you're both after. It can be all too easy for one of you to fall in love, so pay attention to the signs and get ready to move on if things start heading in a direction that you don't want.

Three months seems to be about the maximum amount of time that a fuck-buddy relationship should last. Any longer, and the passion will probably start to fade – and you risk that four-letter word: love. That said, everyone's different so if you're both happy, you can carry on going for longer. Just handle with care.

How to get a fuck buddy

Mentally run through your mates. Are there any who are single and foxy? It may seem obvious, but you could well have discounted someone as a potential conquest because you couldn't see yourself going out with them, neglecting the fuck-buddy option altogether. Things that are an issue in a relationship – say, opposing political beliefs, different lifestyle, weird parents – won't necessarily matter in a fuck-buddy.

Some people find the idea of having sex with an existing mate dreadful; they don't want to potentially ruin any friendship. If so, there may be one-night conquests that can be developed instead. If you've had a fun night with some-one, ask if they'd like to do it again, no strings. The worst that can happen is that they say no. If it's after a heavy night out, don't suggest it until you're sober, though; you might realise you've pulled a swamp-monster in the morn-ing and don't want to commit yourself to any more sex until your beer-goggles have worn off.

The third option is to go out looking for a fuck-buddy. They're not that hard to find; just bring up fuck-buddies as a conversation topic when you're on the pull and, if a guy's into the idea, you'll soon find out. But never guarantee you'll be someone's fuck-buddy until you've fucked them. It's all too easy to suggest it then regret it afterwards, when you realise that you're as sexually compatible as you are with your brother (please don't pursue that line of thought).

Where to go

If you're already mates, go wherever is mutually conven-
ient; you can take him back to your place or go back to
his with far less risk (hopefully) than with a one-night
stand. If you don't know him that well, follow the same
guidelines as with a one-nighter. Fear is a rubbish aphrodisiac, while knowing that you're safe will help you stay
frisky.

What to do

You're in it for a bit of a longer haul, so it's a good time
to try out some of those wilder things that require more
of a degree of trust; power-play, group sex or whatever.
Don't go for these things on day one, though; you may
end up in an ever-escalating list of perversions and at
some stage things are bound to get weird.

If you don't have any kinky ideas – and don't fret,
loads of people don't – then just enjoy good 'vanilla' (ie
'normal') sex. Don't fake orgasm; the point of a fuck-
buddy is for both of you to have great sex. If he's doing
it wrong, show him how to do it right. After all, you've
spent time masturbating, so you know what hits the
spot.

Similarly, ask what he particularly likes. You can never
learn everything about sex because everyone is different, but
experimenting with different partners is one of the easiest
ways to pick up new tricks.

Pros

- Good conversation as well as good sex.
- Calling up and demanding sex (aka, making a booty call) is acceptable so you get what you want more or less when you want.
- Repeatedly shagging the same person gives you a chance to learn about each others' bodies.

Cons

- Risk of losing a friend.
- Risk of falling in love.
- Easily habit-forming and you may be inclined to settle into a relationship that you don't really want.

Filling time with fuck-buddies: Lucy's story

I went through a phase of juggling several fuck-buddies, after I split with my long-term partner, and I had a fantastic time with it. One was a loaded playboy type who took me out to glam places; plying me with champagne; another wasn't really my physical type but had exactly the same mental turn-ons as I did; and another had a great sense of humour and could literally laugh me into bed.

They all knew about each other and were cool with it. I figured that it was better they knew, so that they didn't get involved. There was one point where one of the guys ended up getting a bit jealous, but I soon managed to calm him down by asking whether he'd really like to go out with me. He said that he wouldn't. I didn't keep things going with him for long after that, though; I saw the jealousy as a warning sign.

Having fuck-buddies was OK for a while, but I ended up getting bored with having no-strings sex and decided that I wanted to look for a proper relationship. I wouldn't rule out having a fuck-buddy again in the future though. It's less hassle than one-night stands – I'm not exactly a fan of night clubs and dodgy pulling joints – and I got to live out lots of different fantasies with the various guys.

Better the devil you know?
Sex with an ex

Most people have been there at some stage. One minute, you're feeling proud of yourself for managing to stay friends with the swine who broke your heart, and the next, 'old time's sake' has entered the conversation and your undies have departed the vicinity.

It's so fraught with potential heartbreak that this really isn't one to aim for unless you're really sure that neither of you have any feelings left for each other. The safer option to go 'one-ex-removed'; the person you split up with immediately before your most recent ex. You're both more likely to have moved on so you've got less chance of trauma.

If you do have sex with an ex, don't be surprised if the sex is far better than it was when you were dating. It doesn't mean that you were destined to be together; you're just both likely to be trying harder, and the forbidden element adds spice.

How to get sex with an ex

Sex with an ex is possibly the easiest kind of shag to get, but it's also going back on the past and a bit desperate, so only go for it if the sex was really fantastic. Or you really are desperate.

Generally speaking, if you parted on good terms, all sex with an ex takes is being alone together and having enough alcohol. You know the tricks that work on him so all you have to do is remember them.

Where to go

Your place or his; unless he was always really tight when you went out with him and you like the idea of a night in a flash hotel. A lot of the time, exes will be far nicer to you than they were when you were going out with them because they have to make an effort again, so you can get some payback.

What to do

Settle into the old and comfortable routines or show him how much you've learned since you split up. Be warned that the latter can backfire and lead to a massive row.

Pros

- You know his body and he knows yours.
- You know how to pull him.
- It's safe (assuming you didn't dump him for being a psycho).
- It doesn't add to the numbers (if you're a woman who cares about things like that).

Cons

- One or both of you could still be in love.
- Exes tend to get more jealous if you shag anyone else.
- You can end up feeling that you're only of worth sexually.

Tears before bedtime: Rachel's story

Jim and I split up amicably after two years together. Even though the split was mutual, it was traumatic but, after a month or so of sobbing into my pillow, we started seeing each other as friends. We'd normally go down the pub together and end up the worse for wear. This was all very well, until it came to the time for him to leave at the end of the night. We still had feelings for each other, despite knowing that we didn't work as a couple, and kept ending up in the sack.

The sex was fantastic; far better than it had been when we were together, because there wasn't any of that nagging stuff in the background like 'He hasn't done the washing up'. But it was always really hard to deal with afterwards; he'd go back home and I'd lie in bed, crying.

After a few months of this, we had a break from seeing each other (not intentionally, we just both had other things on). The next time we met up, we had sex but it was different. I'd had sex with other people and realised that, while the sex with him was fine, there wasn't the spark there any more. He seemed to feel the same way, and sex was off the agenda from then on. It made it much easier for us to be friends after we stopped having sex, and now I'd think twice before sleeping with an ex.

Paying for it: using escorts

While about one in ten men have used a prostitute of some type or other, women don't tend to take advantage of the option as much; probably because it's way easier for a woman to get laid than a man. However, it is an option that you may choose to explore if you don't mind breaking the law.

How to get an escort

Classified ads and the internet both come into their own when you're looking for an escort. Depending on what you're after, you can get male escorts, female escorts for women amd even people to join threesomes. Just search online, place your booking and get ready to part with some cash: for 'company' of course.

Where to go

It's safest to meet your escort in a hotel bar. After all, you might not fancy the escort, or you may not want him or her to know where you live. Bear in mind that not all agencies vet their escorts so treat it in the same way as you would meeting a stranger.

What to do

You're paying for it so whatever you want. Just remember that you still need to practice safer sex. Just because an escort is paid for, it doesn't mean that he (or she) will be STI-free.

Pros
- Sex on demand;
- They do what you want them to;
- You can pick what they look like.

Cons
- Illegal;
- Expensive;
- You may end up feeling like you can only get sex if you pay for it.

Bi-curiosity

Over the last few years, the media has got a lot more tolerant about sexuality, and every other day some supermodel seems to be photographed kissing her girlie mate, so it's hardly surprising that today's twenty-something is more likely than ever to have indulged in some lesbian loving. According to a Cliterati poll, over a third of women are bi-curious, in addition to the ten or so per cent who define themselves as lesbian or bisexual.

But with the interest comes the worry. Will the woman you decide to make a move on respond positively? Will you enjoy it? Are you going to have to change sexuality entirely?

There's no need to be scared. Loads of women have had experiences with other women without 'turning into lesbians'. And if you are someone who decides that muff is better than meat, well, what's the harm? Sure, there are still some homophobic idiots around but it's better to be happy in your sexuality than hide who you are and be sad.

It may sound obvious, but don't cop off with another woman if you don't fancy women. Putting on a lesbo show with a woman who fancies you purely to attract men's attention is leading the woman on and taking the piss out of her sexuality purely for your own ends. Then again, if you and a girlie mate both want to pull men by having a bit of a snog, and no-one's getting hurt, it's a pretty safe bet that it'll work (albeit mostly with men whose IQ is even smaller than their penis).

How to get a girl

One of the most common scenarios for bi-curious action is between friends after a few too many drinks and some girlie confessions. One minute, you're talking about the men you fancy, then you're talking about the best time you ever had in the sack and, suddenly, the conversation's moved on to whether you've ever fancied another woman and the temperature in the room is rising.

If you get into this scenario, be careful. Many a friendship has been damaged by a drunken fling. Treat bi-curious experimentation with girlie mates in the same way as you'd treat copping off with a male mate, but be even more wary. Not every woman feels happy with herself after her first same-sex experience and she may take it out on you, or vice versa. Very few fucks are worth losing a friend over.

Instead, wait until you're sober and talk things through. If you decide, in the cold light of day, that you'd still like to go for it (or can even talk to each other about it without blushing) then you can take things from there. If not, you've potentially saved a friendship – and there are plenty more women out there to pull.

Where to go

Sadly, homophobia is alive and well, albeit less overt than it used to be. It's not just in straight bars that you'll face problems. Many lesbian bars are anti-bisexual and bi-curious women, though it's less likely you'll get grief for kissing your date, at least.

However, lesbian bars don't exactly litter the streets unless you're in a fairly large town, so you may find it easiest to stay in together, at your place or hers. It's not that girl/girl action should be hidden behind closed doors but, if you're just going for a brief dip in the pools of pussy, then you may not be prepared to get into a fight about your sexual choice quite yet.

What to do

How long have you got? Much as with straight sex, lesbian sex comes in all kinds of flavours. From fingering to oral sex, fisting to strap-ons, what you get up to is limited only by your imagination. Some common concerns that bi-curious babes have are:

What does a woman taste like?
Well, you've got the bits to taste so stick in a finger and see what it tastes like if you're that concerned. There is a school of thought that blondes, brunettes and redheads taste different from each other, so stick to your same hair colour if you're nervous about encountering something new.

I like the idea of fondling a woman but couldn't go down on one:
So ask the woman concerned if she'd be happy with that

before you go home together. As with any sexual encounter, you don't have to do anything that you don't want to.

What if I'm rubbish at it?
If you check that your partner's enjoying herself all the way through, and ask her to show you what to do if you're not hitting the spot, then you won't be. It's really not all that different from being with a bloke (except for the lack of cock and fact that she'll probably want to talk all night as well).

Pros
- Doubles the opportunity to pull;
- You get to see what it's like to have sex with a woman;
- A lot of men really get the horn if you mention you've had a lesbian experience.

Cons
- Lesbian community is often anti bi-curious women;
- Coming on to girlie mates can be risky;
- Gay-bashing, though less common than it used to be, still happens.

She turned on me: Jane's story

I'd never really thought about copping off with women, until I met Jenny. She was gorgeous; blonde, slim and with a really pretty face. We bonded really quickly, but I just thought that it was as friends. Then, one night, she admitted that she'd had sex with women before. I was curious about it and asked her what it was like. The way she described it was appealing; she said that it was like being with a man but softer and with more touching. I said that I'd never been with a woman before but liked the idea and we'd had a laugh about it. When I got home that night, I ended up masturbating, thinking about her.

From then on, we'd always flirt with each other, and I heard through the grapevine that she'd said she wanted to have sex with me because 'virgins are keen'. Every time she got drunk, she'd make a pass at me, but I was unsure about things. I didn't want to ruin the friendship and, as she was younger than me, I felt weird about taking advantage when she was drunk.

Things came to a head – literally – one night after we'd been to a bar. I'd asked her, earlier on when she was sober, whether she'd meant it when she came on to me when she was drunk, and she'd told me that she did, and that the next time we got drunk, I should go for it. When she made her usual move, I went with it. It felt different kissing her; not as different as I thought it would, but softer and with less stubble. More to the point, I realised that women could turn me on, because I got really aroused.

We started touching each other's breasts and, before long, I was going down on her. Unfortunately, she'd booked a taxi earlier that evening, so she left before I could give her an orgasm. I went to bed feeling happy and wondered when we'd get a chance to take things further.

The next day was horrible, though. I texted her to say thanks for a fun night and she ignored my message. After my repeated attempts to get through to her, she had a massive go at me, accusing me of taking advantage of her. I think that she felt guilty because she had a boyfriend. We'd spent so long – literally months – talking about it that I was certain she'd been up for it.

We ended up losing the friendship over it, and now I'd be very wary about getting off with another woman. Even though the physical experience was enjoyable, the emotional side of things was really unpleasant. I felt like I'd been some kind of abusive bloke, although it did make it easier for me to understand why men sometimes get the wrong signals from women.

Cheating

Casual sex isn't just something for singletons; women who are attached can indulge in it too. Now that's not saying you should – cheating is bad, and you shouldn't do it – but you already know that. Thing is, it happens anyway; about 50 per cent of people are unfaithful to a long-term partner and, in all honesty, they're probably the people who are most in need of casual sex if you throw morals aside. When a couple moves in together – or gets married – their sex life often goes down the drain, and it can seem easier to get laid elsewhere than sort things out at home.

If you cheat, you will make excuses for your behaviour: your partner neglects you; you don't get the kind of sex you want at home, you couldn't resist and all that sort of thing. It's bollocks. You cheat because you want to. If you want to handle things in a mature way, you should tell your partner before you get to the stage where you've cheated and try to work on the problem together, rather than running off and getting your kicks with someone else. Everyone deserves to be with someone who loves them – and is faithful. By cheating, rather than dumping your partner and moving on, you're denying them that opportunity.

But you know all this already. Cheating may not be the right way of dealing with things, but this book's about casual sex, not fixing rubbish partnerships, so get another book if you want to solve your relationship problems.

So, if you're going to cheat, the golden rule is don't get caught. Get a friend to cover for you; one who'll say 'She was with me' and ask you questions later. Make sure she doesn't fancy your man, though, or you might find her taking advantage of your indiscretion to get jiggy with him.

When you're seeing your bit on the side, never pay for anything by credit card, or do anything else that leaves a paper trail. He should call you, but never on your land-line, or he could leave a message on the answerphone that makes your partner suspicious. And make sure that the person you're screwing on the side knows that you're attached, or he could inadvertently drop you in it.

If you learn some tip or technique in the sack from your new partner, don't show your live-in lover without a damn good excuse (eg 'I read about X in a magazine. Could we try it?'), otherwise he'll get suspicious. Ditto buying new lingerie. If you're going to get it, take your long-term partner with you. Yes, it's sleazy buying undies with one guy to wear with another, but affairs are sleazy. Deal with it.

And if you – or the guy you're seeing – starts to get attached, cut it dead immediately. Either that, or dump the man you're with long-term. Very few people can manage multiple-love relationships (that's a whole other book) and it's the easiest way to get your heart broken and mess up your love-life.

Where to go

Anywhere you won't get caught. Never even consider having sex at your place. Not only is it in poor taste, but you really don't want to get stuck in some 'hiding a man in the cupboard' farce.

What to do

Be very careful. Make sure that you don't get into wild sex with biting and scratching because you're going to get caught. And if you're doing a woman on the side, watch out for lipstick on your collar.

It should go without saying, but make extra sure that you practise safer sex, particularly if you and your long-term partner have been tested for STIs and don't use condoms any more. It's bad enough that you're cheating on the poor sod; you don't want to give him an STI too.

Pros
- Can be exciting.
- Can put a relationship back on track; some people try harder after an affair's ended.
- Can make you appreciate your partner more, when you realise that other men out there have just as many bad habits.

Cons
- Could end your long-term relationship.
- Can make you feel really guilty.
- All that stuff you see on *Oprah*; getting pregnant by 'the wrong' man, giving your long-term guy an STI and numerous other fun things.

I still regret it: Katva's story

I'd been with Che for seven years and our sex life had dwindled so that it was practically non-existent. I tried everything – asking for sex, not asking for sex, dancing around in skimpy underwear, putting porn videos on – but nothing worked. I began to feel really ugly and like I was utterly worthless.

Around this time an old flame, Andy, got back in touch with me. He'd moved to the area and when he called, asking if I wanted to meet up – as friends – I was more than happy to. We'd always got on well and it had been an amicable break-up – he'd just moved to another town.

We ended up talking until the early hours and when I realised I'd missed the last train home, Andy said I could crash on the sofa. I called Che, who said it was fine, and Andy and I carried on talking. As the wine bottle grew emptier, the whole story came out; how little sex I got, how unattractive I felt – and when I started crying, Andy gave me a hug. It felt so nice being held that I found myself kissing him.

To his credit, Andy stopped me and asked if I was sure that it was what I wanted; he didn't want to mess anything up even though he really wanted me. After being pushed away every time I'd initiated sex with Che for the last few years, knowing that another man wanted me was enough to make me certain. I nodded, and we ended up having sex on the floor. It was fantastic; it made me feel desired again, and it felt like I was doing the right thing.

The next morning, the guilt set in. I didn't tell Che what I'd done, though, and Andy and I fell into having an affair; the sex was too addictive not to. It was incredible but confusing. I wasn't sure whether I should leave Che – I loved him – whereas I knew that things would never work with Andy, but the sex was exactly what I needed.

After a couple of months, the guilt got too much for me. I confessed all to Che, and he asked whether I wanted to leave him. I said no, and that I'd stopped seeing Andy and wouldn't ever do it again, because Che was too important to me.

For a while afterwards, things were better – Che made an effort, and I began to feel happier with him – but it turned out that he couldn't handle me having had an affair. He ended up running off with a mate of mine who he'd confided to about my infidelity. I still regret what I did to this day, and wonder if things would have worked with Che if I hadn't cheated.

Being a mistress

Being a mistress has the same moral issues as cheating on a partner, but it's the person who's attached that should take the bulk of the responsibility, because they're the one breaking a promise to someone they claim to love. If you want no-strings fun then you may decide that being a mistress is the way forward. However, bear in mind that only one per cent of men leave their wife for their mistress, so be damned sure that you're not going to fall in love. It's easy to underestimate the thrills that you can get from doing something forbidden, so handle with extreme care.

It's also worth remembering that, if your affair is discovered, you're the one who'll be blamed for leading the man astray. Just look at what happened with Beckham and his alleged affair; he was considered blameless while

Rebecca Loos and Posh were both lambasted by the press. Yep, it's sexist but that's life. You'll be considered a wanton hussy and not in a good way.

If you're a mistress, you won't have any of the power in the relationship; you can't call your man if you feel sad (or horny) and will have to take whatever spare time the guy is prepared to give you, without complaining. And, contrary to the glam image of being a mistress, not that many men can afford diamonds and nights in chic hotels. Do you really want to spend your nights fucking in seedy motels because he knows that his wife won't know anyone there? Or worse, getting a quick shag after he finishes work, then watching him dash back to his wife?

Where to go

Anywhere you won't get caught. Never go to his place – it's far too dangerous. Similarly, make sure you don't go anywhere near his house, his parent's house, his wife's best mate's house, his wife's work, his wife's favourite café or – well – anywhere really. Even your house can be risky, if he's seen going into it; you don't want an irate wife turning up on your doorstep (or worse).

So, that leaves you with motels on the outskirts of town or, if he has an understanding mate, the mate's flat. Be very careful though: unless you're a bitch, you don't want to break another woman's heart and, if you're going to shag her bloke, the least she deserves is not to know.

What to do

Be damned careful. Don't scratch him or bite him. Check his clothes for your hairs before he leaves you and don't wear lipstick or perfume that could make his wife suspicious.

Pros

- You can get a thrill out of doing something forbidden.
- He might treat you like a goddess because he feels so guilty about cheating.
- It's totally no-strings.

Cons

- He's got all the control in the relationship.
- You're indirectly hurting another woman.
- You may well not be the only one – other than his wife – he's having sex with.
- He may take his guilt out on you.
- Married men almost never leave their wives.

He lied: Emma's story

I first met Greg on the train home from a party in London. He stared at me without talking for the entire journey and gave me his business card as he got off. We spoke on the phone a few days later and arranged to meet.

Just before the date I received an e-mail from him telling me that he was married but that his marriage had problems. I didn't know what to do. Attached men were completely out of bounds to me. However, I had just wasted more than a decade of my life struggling in a marriage that was dead so I felt I needed to find out more before I judged the situation.

At the end of that first date I was completely smitten, which is very rare for me. He gave me the impression that his marriage was doomed. The truth came out a couple of months later; his marriage was fine and he still loved his wife. I was horrified and from that moment on tried to excise him from my life – but by then I was too hooked.

I was never cut out to be a mistress. I couldn't accept that the man I loved went from my bed to that of the woman he chose to spend his life with and I had conspired in deceiving her. The only good part was that the excitement never had a chance to die and nearly two years on we still wanted each other as much as we did on that first date. I'd never be a mistress again though, and would warn any woman off it too. It's just too heartbreaking.

Casual relationships

Casual sex often masquerades in relationship-form. You're dating someone, they're kind of nice, you might want to go out with them long term or you might not but, while they're there, you may as well take advantage.

However, you want to avoid breaking hearts so, if you're pretty sure that you're not after anything serious, make sure you're clear about it from day one. Explain that you like him and enjoy his company but aren't in a position to look for love right now because [insert excuse of choice here]. Good excuses include getting over your ex (don't elaborate or you'll turn the guy off), needing to keep a distance because you're going travelling/may be moving to another town soon (don't use it if it's not true or he'll spot you in your local a week after you break up) and needing to focus on your career.

As long as you're honest — and he's not a bunny-boiler — you should be able to keep things fun and friendly, enjoying the 'relationship' for what it is. Do let him know if you start to fall in love, though; it's not fair to say one thing and do another — and broken hearts are no fun at all.

Pros
- You get to go out on dates.
- You can experiment with each other in a safe environment.
- You can take him home to meet your mum.

Cons
- You could end up settling for someone you don't really fancy.
- You could end up falling in love with someone who doesn't want you.
- It could get dull.

Free love at what cost? Rosie's story

My longest casual sex affair was with Sam, who I met at a festival and copped off with. When I say sex, it mostly ended up being conducted via text. Due to our commitments it was three months before we could meet up so in that time we texted regularly. One night I told him I had just got out of the bath. He asked me if I was naked. I said I was, and that I was steaming the windows up. A couple of texts later and my hand was between my legs and my windows were white with mist! We kept this up for months; at least once a week we'd spend up to five hours a night having text sex and when we met ... it was phenomenal. We didn't do anything but have sex; we accidentally pulled the curtains down, we stained my chair with cum, we did every position that was humanly possible. It was such a great period in my sex life; Sam and I were both sleeping with other people but could also text or call each other when we needed a fix during a 'dry patch'!

Until he stopped replying. Out of nowhere he stopped answering my calls, and didn't reply to my text messages. I was really upset at first, I didn't know what had happened to make him ignore me. But I got over it and then, two months later, he texted me to apologise, saying he'd had a lot of stuff happen in his life but he still loved me. This was news to me, as he'd never said he loved me in the first place, but it drew me right back in. I wanted him wanting me. My friends had started being a bit wary of the situation but I told them not to worry, it was only a casual thing.

For a while it was great, back to how it had been, but before long he called me to say there was someone else he was especially keen on. I was supposed to be visiting him that week and he said we could still meet and catch up. Predictably, we ended up sleeping together and the next day I had to pretend not to know him as he dropped me off at the same station the other girl was due to meet him at. I loved the naughtiness of it; it was so exciting. We were bohemian love children enjoying each other; what could be wrong with that? However, after he dropped me off I didn't hear from him again.

I said to myself that this was cool, it was just a casual thing, and before long started seeing someone seriously. And then, six months later, I bumped into Sam again at a festival. He smiled at me. My heart raced, I could hardly breathe. I didn't know what to do. He was coming on to me and I told him I couldn't play around with him any more because I had a boyfriend, but I was really struggling. He had stopped seeing the other girl; in fact the last time he had seen her was the same day that he had stopped seeing me. He was sorry he hadn't been in touch but he had had a lot of stuff to deal with. He told me he loved me.

Our friends were convinced we were getting up to mischief when they weren't around because we kept going off for long walks together but all we were doing was talking and holding hands. I was holding it together despite my whole body aching for him, wanting him inside me. He told me he loved me again, twice. I tried to ignore it. This lasted until the last night. His friends were thinking of leaving that night to beat the traffic so we were saying goodbye. I couldn't bear it any longer and beckoned him to follow me to the side of a nearby portacabin, where no-one could see us. He looked bewildered. I grabbed his T-shirt, pulled him to me and we grappled like we needed each other to breathe, kissing so hungrily, gasping for breath, groping throbbing crotches. I was determined no-one should know so after five minutes of kissing we emerged, stumbling from the darkness before anyone came looking for us. Before we parted he told me he loved me again. I said I loved him too.

After he left I was distraught. I knew he was totally unreliable, I knew he would never be a faithful boyfriend to me (and although I love the idea of free love, if I'm serious about a relationship then I am faithful and expect the same in return). I had a boyfriend I loved and who loved me but ... oh I wanted Sam so badly.

In the end I confessed the snog to my boyfriend, weeping all over the both of us. He asked me if I wanted to be with Sam and I said no. He said he forgave me but I couldn't stop crying, I felt so sorry I had treated my boyfriend so badly but, if I'm honest, I was also crying because I was sorry to have to accept the impossibility of a relationship with Sam, mourning the loss of all the breathtakingly amazing sex we had together.

Sam contacted me a couple of times afterwards but it was never the same once I wouldn't be sexual with him. In time I realised that he'd only ever said he loved me when he wanted me to sleep with him. But that's not the real lesson I learnt from the affair. For me, it signalled the waning of my interest in being into free love to that degree. I learned that for me there was no such thing as free love. It was always buy now, pay later.

Chapter 4

How to Pull Anyone

Now you know the kind of casual sex you're looking for, all you need to do is get it. This is the part that most people freak out about, but it's dead easy, if you approach it in the right way. The important mantra to repeat to yourself, scrawl on your mirror and absorb as part of your inner psyche is this: men are easy to pull.

'Rubbish,' you say. 'I haven't had sex for months and I've been trying really hard.' Then you've been trying in the wrong way.

Much as I loathe clichés, the idea of a man being up for sex most of the time is, broadly speaking, true. Most single men, when offered it on a plate, will say yes. Or rather, drool 'yes' while hailing a taxi to whisk you back to his place before you change your mind, and unbuttoning his flies with his spare hand.

The approach laid out in this chapter has worked on almost every kind of man: male models, shy-boys, DJs, porn stars, geeks, dancers, high-flying businessmen, students, TV execs and almost anything you could imagine in between. It's worked for women of all shapes and sizes and has nothing to do with physical attractiveness. It's just about having that 'fuck me' attitude, and being unafraid to ask for what you want.

Preparing the ground

Before you even go out on the pull, you need to make sure that you haven't got any 'barriers to entry'. (OK, it's a marketing term but it seems somewhat fitting.) You don't want to move in for the kill on your lusty lothario then lose momentum and sparkle, as you remember that you're wearing your period pants or have left the flat in a state that's more conducive to penicillin experimentation than seduction.

Start by making sure your abode is in a suitable state to bring someone back to. Run through the following checklist before you leave the house for a night out to avoid embarrassment:

Is there any evidence of other men?
It's all very well being into brief encounters, but you don't want the bloke you bring home to think you do this all the time. Even if your behaviour's left him in no doubt as to

the kind of girl you really are, if your room is littered with used condoms and tissues from the guy you had round last night, you may find that it ruins the mood. Don't get me wrong; casual sex is nothing to be ashamed of, but you'd think a bloke was a bit cheap if you walked into his room to find it littered with another woman's underwear. Either that, or kinky.

Similarly, cups or glasses on both sides of the bed, rather than just one, can suggest that, no matter what you say, you do do this all the time. And it should go without saying that you should have clean sheets; sleeping on a wet patch that you've created together is one thing, but expecting a bloke to sleep on a wet patch created by another guy is tasteless. And only a little bit funny.

A grim surprise: Anna's story

I was round at a fuck-buddy's house and we were getting down to it, missionary-style, on the bed. After a while, we moved into spooning position and, from my changed vantage-point, I noticed a used condom lying next to the bed. I wouldn't have minded, but we didn't use condoms, so I knew that it was from someone else. I wasn't really that keen to continue after I'd seen that. Even though I knew he fucked other people, I didn't want my nose – almost literally – rubbed in the proof.

Do you have coffee, alcohol and painkillers in the house?

Inviting someone in for coffee, then not having any, can be a touch embarrassing and will probably result in less foreplay; the joy of having a coffee with someone is that you get to spend time kissing and chatting while you drink it, rather than just leaping straight into bed and skipping the all-important anticipation. Having alcohol in the house is always handy, too, as you can use it as a ploy to lure someone back after the pubs have closed.

As to the painkillers, well, if there's alcohol involved, it's always best to be on the safe side. While orgasm does serve to get rid of headaches, if your head is throbbing with an alcohol-induced migraine then you'll probably find it far trickier to come.

Do you have anything embarrassing on display?

If your bedside table is full of books such as '*How to get a man*', '*How to meet Mr Right*' or even this book, it could put the poor guy off before you've had a chance to sample the contents of his boxers. Similarly, a bed covered with cuddly toys could make him run away screaming, fearing that you're a bunny-boiler or trying far too hard to cling on to your cute and girlie side.

Other things to avoid having on display include photos of ex boyfriends, any personal letters (he'll read them the second you go to the loo), thrush cream and other embarrassing pharmaceuticals. Depending on how open-minded you are, you may want to stow away any dirty books that you're reading. Then again, you might want to read him an inspiring 'bedtime story', so that one's entirely your call.

Is the answering machine set to pick up without playing the message audibly?

Imagine the scene; you're there, hands wandering with abandon over his six-pack, knowing that, any second now, you're going to be getting naked when 'Brrrrring', the phone goes, and your mother is there leaving you a message about her operation or, worse, another guy you've pulled is calling for phone sex. Hardly likely to set the mood. So turn it down; or even unplug the phone. I mean, you wouldn't answer it during sex, anyway, would you? *Would* you?

Added bonuses

While it's by no means essential, if you want to have the ultimate casual sex, it's worth paying a bit of attention to your boudoir. Scented candles and incense will give the room a pleasant aroma and sexy ambience. Investing in stylish sheets will help you feel like a sex goddess (and they don't need to be that expensive). You can find satin bedding relatively inexpensively and you'll feel like Mata Hari when you curl up underneath it.

Getting your favourite sexy CDs out is a good idea, as it will save time later. And have a 'sex box' next to the bed, containing condoms, lube and anything else that you're likely to need in the course of getting it on. You might not want your vibrators in there, though; at least not until you've had time to establish whether he's the kind of boy who's happy to play with toys.

Preparing yourself
Bathing beauty

Now that your flat looks gorgeous, it's time to put the work in on yourself. Pour yourself a glass of wine, run a bath and get ready for some serious pampering. It's not mere sybaritic indulgence – well, OK, the wine is – it's an essential part of your seduction set-up. You're aiming to attract a man the second you walk into a bar, or wherever, just from the way that you smell.

Never underestimate the importance of aroma; it's a massive part of seduction. You're naturally attracted to men whose pheromones (smell hormones) indicate they have complementary immune systems to yours, and vice versa, so that you have healthy babies (even if you're not at that 'baby-making' stage). See, you thought that feeling horny at the way a man smells was just down to nice aftershave, but it's actually biology.

Although your natural pheromones will be utterly intoxicating to the right bloke, sweat just isn't stylish. Instead, go for a classier approach with aphrodisiac aromatherapy oils, such as sandalwood and ylang ylang, or get scientific about it and go with scents that make him stiff. Studies by Dr Alan Hirsch of the Smell and Taste Research Foundation have found that men are most physically aroused by the smell of pumpkin pie, liquorice, doughnuts or lavender. You may not be able to get pumpkin pie-flavoured shower-gel (then again, almost anything is possible nowadays) but lavender is easy enough to get hold of. Or, if you're into older men, go for vanilla; it apparently gives them the horn more than anything else.

Having chosen the perfume you'll use to pull, and scented your bath, get in and start buffing. Soft skin feels better to the touch, so you'll be more likely to get a man stroking you all over, when you get him in the sack. Body-buffing gloves are a great alternative to expensive exfoliation products; they don't make the bath all gritty and can be used with whatever shower gel or soap you like best.

Now, to shave or not to shave? While stubbly legs are unappealing to most blokes and are probably best kept silky smooth, body hair is a personal choice. You don't need to feel obliged to have a Brazilian or pube-free pudenda; indeed, a fair few men prefer a woman with natural pubes. Added to this, both pubic hair and armpit hair are full of pheromones, so the more you shave off, the more you reduce your body's natural pulling perfume.

The boring bit:
Making sure you don't get up the duff

While having children can be a wonderful thing, chances are you don't want to get pregnant when you're shagging around. You should always use a condom anyway, to help avoid STIs but sometimes the little buggers split, so it's worth having a back-up to prevent all the horridness that comes with a pregnancy scare.

Contraception choices?

The pill

Some women love it and others hate it. If you're a depressive kind of girl then it may not be the best option, as it can make even the sanest woman weepy. And if you're a smoker, talk to your doctor as you shouldn't have certain kinds of pill. Generally, the pill is believed to protect against some cancers but increase the risk of others. It can improve skin quality but can also cause weight gain, loss of sex drive (ironically) and a variety of other symptoms. Read the leaflet inside your pill packet and talk to your doctor if you have any concerns.

The coil

While some women find it an effective solution, the coil doesn't always implant in the body properly and it can lead to heavier periods. It's usually something for women in stable relationships, as it can exacerbate certain STIs.

The cap or diaphragm

Other than its habit of 'pinging' across the room at inopportune moments, the cap can also be messy and cut down on spontaneity when you fiddle around trying to get it in. It should be used with a spermicide, so you also might get slimy hands. Oh, and if you're prone to cystitis, avoid it like the plague. It can make your attacks more frequent.

Withdrawal

You're having a laugh aren't you? Firstly, think of the STIs the bloke could have. And secondly, withdrawal isn't a reliable method of contraception as sperm is contained in pre-cum, the fluid that leaks out of a bloke's cock before he comes. Yep, there are over three million sperm on the head of a cock even before he's come – and it only takes one to get you pregnant. Don't be an idiot. OK?

Femidom

Although as a barrier form of contraception it can help protect against STIs, the Femidom looks like a windsock and sounds like the shopping being brought in. Some women may find it difficult to insert. However, it can be used to give you an orgasm if you rub the ring against your clit, so it's worth trying once to see if that makes up for it.

Hormone implants

These can be good for women who tend to forget to take the pill every day, but can cause similar side-effects. That said, it's a lower dosage than the pill, which has got to be a good thing.

Morning-after pill

This shouldn't be used as a regular form of contraception as it's effectively an ultra-high dose of the pill (but never take a whole packet of the regular pill instead; it doesn't work). However, if a condom splits then it's better to play it safe. You can now get the morning-after pill from the chemist. If you have to pay for it, tap the bloke for half the money; after all, it's his tadpoles that caused the problem and it's cheaper than child support! Contrary to what the name suggests, the morning-after pill can actually be used up to 72 hours after you have sex – and the latest version can even be used up to 120 hours after (though the sooner you take it, the better).

The only 100 per cent effective method is abstinence, but that's no fun at all. However, combining a condom with one of the methods above (excluding the Femidom, which is a barrier method itself) will increase the odds of staying baby-free.

If you're keeping your pubes au naturel, just give them a quick wash with shampoo and even condition them so that they stay nice and soft, then comb them through when you get out the bath to get rid of any 'stragglers' that could get caught in a guy's throat when he's going down on you.

You may want to shave the bikini line to keep things looking trim when you're wearing skimpy knickers. If you want to get really flash, you can now get pubic-shaping kits and trim your muff into anything from a lightening bolt to a heart. And some women are 'Caribbean' addicts who want to remove the lot. Whatever; if you are going to shave your pubes at all, use lukewarm rather than hot water to lather up. It won't open the pores as much, so you've got less danger of getting dry skin and itchy grow-back. And when you get out of the bath, slather on lots of moisturiser designed for sensitive skin to further minimise shaving rash.

Body-confidence

Once you're all bathed and scented with seductive oils, decide what you're going to wear. While inner beauty is all very well, most people are shallow, so looking your best is important. Luckily, anyone can look fantastic with enough confidence and the right clothes. Pretty much every woman has at least one bodily feature to be proud of, so show yours off. Not sure what your ultimate asset is? Think back on all the compliments you've ever had. Yes, it's much easier to remember insults but forget about being all reserved and self-deprecating; if you want to pull, you need to ooze self-confidence and know exactly how sexy you are.

After boosting your confidence with the memories of all those compliments, look at yourself naked in the mirror. Rather than fixating on your lumps and bumps, see which bits you think are best. It could be a part of your body – buttocks, legs or whatever – or it could be a facial feature. Whatever it is, make sure that you emphasise it; if you're trying to land a catch then you need to bait the hook with something appetising.

Fashion for passion

The perfect pulling outfit doesn't need to be expensive, just flatteringly designed to highlight your best features. If you're not sure which outfit shows you off to your ultimate advantage, ask your mates – particularly any straight male mates — what you look sexiest in. As a broad rule, men don't care about fashion, so forget about what's in or out and think about what makes you feel gorgeous.

By far the most important thing is to wear whatever you feel happiest in. It's far better to be your natural and lovely self than to try to conform to any stereotypes. But there are a few clothing tricks that you can try to use to your advantage.

The perfect pulling outfit starts with your underwear. Wearing lovely lingerie will make you look sexier, even when no one else can see it. Silk skanties will rub against your skin, giving you sensual thrills all day. And if you feel more seductive and desirable, you'll be more seductive and desirable. Plus, if you do pull, you won't have to worry about what you're wearing underneath. On which note, if you own any knickers that are past their best — greying, stained or whatever — bin them right now. If you own them, you'll be tempted to wear them, and sod's law means that you're bound to pull when you do. So chuck them out, or maybe even take them into the garden and burn them ceremonially. If it all goes horribly wrong, you could end up with a load of firemen pawing through your knickers, and if you can't take advantage of an opportunity like that then you really need to tune in your shag-radar.

Once your lingerie is sorted, you can move onto the stuff on top. When it comes to outer-wear, men tend to like flashes of flesh — and that's flashes, not swathes — so forget clothes that leave nothing to the imagination. You may only want to get laid, but you don't want him to think you're a slut. If he does, he'll skip foreplay, assuming that he can get away with it. Either that, or you'll be so busy fending off losers who fancy any woman who's flashing flesh that you'll miss out on the fit but shyer guy who can breathe through his ears.

Go for the old trick of balancing your outfit. If you've got great tits, flash the cleavage but wear trousers or a long skirt. If you've got gorgeous legs, go for a micromini but team it with a polo-neck top. Leaving something to the imagination will mean that a man spends time mentally undressing you, making it far easier for you to lure him back for a night of passion.

It's not just your style of outfit that matters. The right fabric can make a difference, too. Pick something that's soft and strokeable so that your lust object is dying to run his fingers all over your body. Cashmere, or lambswool as a cheaper equivalent, is a good bet, as is silk, satin (but not stretch-satin trousers unless you have an incredibly good arse – anything but the perfect peach will look awful in them) and anything (fake) furry.

My coat got me laid: Alyson's story

When I was a student, I had a fake fur jacket that felt unbelievably fluffy. Whenever I wore it out, men would ask if they could stroke it because it looked so snuggly. Obviously, I'd only let cute guys stroke it – if they bought me a drink.

That jacket was responsible for more shags than anything else that I own, and even though it's far too tatty to wear now – probably from all that stroking – I couldn't bear to throw it away. It's got far too many sexy memories attached.

Colour is also important. According to Colour Consultant Leatrice Eiseman, director of the Pantone Colour Institute and author of *Colours For Your Every Mood*, pink-peach is the most attractive colour to men. It makes women seem approachable, flatters most skin tones by giving you a healthy glow and (get ready to have your feminist hackles raised) makes women appear vulnerable, which brings out men's protective instinct.

If that's just too offensive a concept for you, go for red, burgundy or plum. Apparently, men who dislike strong women will avoid you if you wear these colours. As well as weeding out wusses, wearing red acts as a good short-hand for 'fuck me now'; it's the colour representing sex and power and attracts men who want sex (yeah, OK, that's all of them) or like powerful women (you do have some thigh-boots and a whip, don't you?). The ultimate turn-off colour is what Eiseman calls 'squished caterpillar yellow-green'. It repels men and women equally. But who'd want to wear that anyway?

Jewellery can also be a useful pulling tool. According to research, men rate women wearing long earrings as more sensual. And a necklace can act as a 'look here' arrow, if you have top tits. You may also want to invest in a pair of stick-on nipples (or just pinch yours every time you go to the toilet, so that they stay perky). Men, being visual beasts, will be drawn to your pert peanuts and want to have a nibble.

Make-out make-up

You smell right, you're dressed to kill; now all you need is the war-paint. As with your clothes, fashion should have no place in your make-up if you're after sex. Instead, use make-up to emphasise your assets. Don't put your make-up on with a trowel, though. Most men don't like a woman who's caked in the stuff.

Shockingly, according to research, men find sensual lips more of a turn-on than big breasts: lips are the second thing that a bloke looks for when he's clocking a woman (the first being athletic body shape). Lips are a turn-on for men because they offer a 'genital echo' by subconsciously representing the labia; they even expand, like labia do when you're aroused. As a result, the fuller and redder your lips are, the more they resemble aroused labia and the hotter you'll seem (ain't psychology grand?). So pick a lipstick that's close to your natural lip-colour but with a red tone. Lip-gloss is obviously a good thing, too, as it makes your lips look wet …

Eyes are another important factor when it comes to pulling a man, coming in at number seven in their fave foxy features. The bigger your eyes look, the better, as it suggests youthfulness, something that men are biologically drawn to. Invest in a pair of eyelash curlers as they'll make your eyes look bigger, as will the right mascara and eyeliner.

And men may not make passes at girls who wear glasses, but wearing contact lenses boosts your pulling chances above those of women with 20:20 vision. Contacts make the pupils dilate and the eyes glisten, both things that indicate arousal. The most popular eye-colour with men is blue, and generally light-coloured eyes are seen as more attractive, so a pair of tinted contacts could also make it easier to land your catch.

Face powder and foundation will help even your skin tone, which adds to the youthful thing and suggests you have good genes (making him want to get into your jeans). And, finally, don't forget the blusher; your skin flushes when you're aroused, so you're sending out yet another 'I'm gagging for it, me' message – never a bad thing if you're looking for sex.

Let the hunt begin

Now you've laid the groundwork, it's time to get laid. For that, fairly obviously, you need to find a man. While it can sometimes seem like an impossible quest, there are over 11 million singles in the UK and over 80 million singles in the US. They can't all be staying at home every night. So if you want a brief encounter, get out there and play the numbers game: the more people you meet, the more likely you are to pull. Remember, though, the objective is to find someone you'd like to get into the sack, not simply to find someone who'd like to get you into it. Don't throw your standards out the window. After all, the person you choose gets to sleep with you, so they need to be worthy of a sex-goddess, right? Decide what you're after, then go out and get it.

What to take: your essential brief encounter kit

You're almost ready to leave the house now but, first, make sure that your handbag has got all your essentials in it (and that's not just phone, purse and keys). Be prepared, or so the old motto goes, and never is it truer than for casual sex. You never know where your next shag will come from, so make sure you've always got the following on you and you'll always be ready for action:

- *The telephone number of a taxi company*: You never know where you'll end up or if you'll want to make a speedy exit. Ideally, find a firm that takes credit cards so that, even if you're out of cash, you can still get home safely.

- *Condoms*: It's always best to have a selection of brands and sizes. Condomi are good for the smaller man and Trojan Magnums are great for the well-endowed hunk. Keep them in a condom case to prevent them from getting damaged when they're in your wallet or bag.

- *Lube*: Not just for anal action, lube makes hand-jobs easier and can also double for condom-safe massage oil. Some brands come in individual sachets, which are far more portable than tubes or tubs.

- *Make-up*: If you wear make-up then always carry the essentials with you. You don't want the entire office to know you got lucky.

- *Clean knickers*: A thong will fit into the smallest bag and means that you've always got something sexy to slip into the next morning.

- *A toothbrush or chewing gum*: So you can smell minty-fresh.

- *Facial cleansing wipes and deodorant wipes*: So you don't wake up with a massive zit and go into work all stinky.

- *Hangover cure*: Men are generally rubbish at having well-stocked medicine cabinets and Cosmopolitans are far more enjoyable the night before than the morning after.
- *A-Z streetmap or equivalent*: So that, no matter where you end up, you can still get home easily.
- *Anything else you can't live without*: For some people, this is contact lens solution, for others, it's as simple as a cup of coffee. Get those individual sachets of coffee, whitener and sugar and you'll never have to cope with the morning after sans caffeine again.

Instinctive attraction: Jemma's approach

My take on casual sex has always been to sleep only with people who I'm 'instinctively attracted' to. It's there or it's not, end of story. I've never been a 'go-home-with-the-best-looking-guy-left-at-the-end-of-the-night' girl. This approach has meant accepting that it might be months before the next person I'm instinctively attracted to comes along, and waiting till that happens (I've never waited more than three months, though, and usually it's taken much less time; twice in one day being the quickest).

The result, however, has been that I've only ever had fab casual sex; sex that everyone's enjoyed, where I've felt safe and happy and uninhibited, where there's been no embarrassment next morning/afternoon, that I've never regretted, and that has always been repeated at least once. The exception was the one time I broke my own rule and took someone home because he was textbook-fit and I was horny, but the 'instinctive' thing wasn't there, and it was awful.

Without getting too much into psycho-babble, one tried-and-tested technique for attracting the right kind of person is 'positive visualisation', a pseudo-scientific sounding phrase for what basically equates to 'writing a list'.

Get a pen and paper (or computer — there's no arcane law about these things) and list the attributes you're looking for. These could be physical things (such as blonde hair, nice eyes, or buttocks you couldn't *not* bite if you had it in range), material attributes (a flash car, say, or a slick bachelor pad) or personality traits (for example, 'kind' or 'chatty' or 'not a whiny freeloader').

You can also put traits that you don't want on the list, for example, 'alcoholic' or 'druggie'. Both are best avoided, not least because your evening of sizzling sex is likely to turn into nothing but listening to some guy talk about how rubbish his life is until he throws up and then falls asleep with his head resting on the toilet seat. Even if he does focus on you, erections don't tend to behave when they're being driven by a man with a loaded system.

Read your lust list regularly (add to it, if more attributes spring to mind) and, as if by magic, you'll start to attract people who are 'your type'. Really, you *will*. Athletes and psychologists use variations of this technique to help improve achievement or boost self-esteem, so there's loads of evidence to back up the theory. You may only be after a night of hot action, but it's much more fun if you get to enjoy the time before and after you get down to it as well.

Rampant action without risk

If you're regularly going out on the pull, rest assured that you'll run into a fair few idiot men. Some are masters of disguise who can masquerade as nice guys until the point at which you get them home, so you need to make sure your tosser-radar is tuned in if you want to avoid hassle.

First off, listen to your gut instinct. Women's intuition well and truly exists, so make sure that you pay attention to yours. If a bloke is gorgeous and interesting but makes you feel uncomfortable, don't ignore the vibes you're getting. It's not a load of hippy rubbish; you're probably picking up on subconscious signals that the man's sending out. Make your excuses and move on.

If a bloke gets aggressive when someone knocks into him or whatever, leave well alone. He could end up getting aggressive with you, which is no fun at all. Conversely, if a man who you've just met tells you that he could fall in love with you, avoid him like the plague. Not only will he be harder to get rid of than chewing gum on your little black dress the morning after, but he could also turn stalker on you.

He made my life hell: Antonia's story

Typical story: I met a guy in a club. We clicked; we had sex a couple of times. It meant nothing to me, but he found himself wanting a lot more than a few brief encounters. I told him I didn't feel the same and that I thought we should just be friends.

He then became very chummy with my other mates and always found out where I was hanging out. The crunch came when he turned up at a pub where I was having birthday drinks. He was completely plastered and literally followed me around, standing between me and all my friends all night until I eventually went home, emotionally exhausted.

After that, I refused to speak to him again and his behaviour grew worse. He left up to 50 abusive messages a day on my land and mobile lines, he came to my house and tried to kick my door down, he attacked friends' cars when they were parked in my driveway and he threw books about serial killers over my garden fence. He even went as far as posting messages online about me being unprofessional. I have quite a high-profile job and I love my work, so for me this was the final straw.

Ultimately for him, casual sex led to a formal warning from the police. The threat of a court case finally put a stop to his freakish behaviour but, despite my brave face, for months afterwards I was terrified of seeing him staring at me through my window, or hearing his boot on my door.

The old line 'do you fancy a drink?' is best rebuffed too, because, sadly, drink spiking is on the increase. Some men use Rohypnol, the 'date rape' drug, while others go for recreational drugs such as Ecstasy to make you feel loved up and lower your resistance. Not only can this put you at risk of ending up in a threatening situation with a stranger, but it can also be potentially lethal if you react badly to the drug, so guard your drink at all times. It may sound like a pain, but don't let a bloke buy you a drink unless you know him well and, even then, be careful, as acquaintance rape – where you know the guy – is increasingly common.

If you do let a man you don't know buy you a drink, go to the bar with him and have a bottle rather than a glass, making sure that you watch when it's opened. Take the bottle directly from the barman to reduce the chances of your man slipping something into it – and watch the barman too, as some sick individuals work as a double act with a friend behind the bar when drugging women. While it sounds boring being so cautious, it's better to be safe than raped.

I didn't know what happened: Monica's story

I had my drink spiked one Friday night when I was out with a group of friends in town. One minute I was fine, talking to a friend, the next I was tottering around, feeling really ill and bouncing off the walls to get to the bathroom, where it took all my strength and will power not to pass out.

I knew straight away that something wasn't right. I'd only had a couple of glasses of champagne all night. I managed to drag myself back into the main club area to find my friends and tell them we had to leave.

A male friend had to literally carry me up the stairs and out of the club and into a taxi. I threw up on the way home and can't remember anything after getting back. Apparently I was really aggressive, shouting and fighting, and he made me have a cold shower before I totally passed out on the bed (I have no recollection of this). The next morning I felt sick, with slight hallucinations, very dazed and incredibly drained.

Looking back, I can remember a weird, dark-haired man sitting on my left trying to talk to us. My friend and I both thought he was a bit odd and didn't pay much attention.

The club, to give them credit, were great. I reported it to them and they were apologetic and said they'd be on their guard. The frightening thing is that this was the third time it had happened there, and they still didn't know who was doing it. However, they seemed to think that it was someone doing it for fun, rather than for more sinister reasons.

Often the guy who spikes your drink waits outside the toilet for you to emerge, dazed and disorientated, verging on unconsciousness and wanting to go home, then escorts you out of the club, saying he'll make sure you get home okay. Club security is usually glad to see the back of anyone who appears out of control or drunk. Then you pass out, not being able to remember anything that's happened.

A friend I spoke with was spiked once. She ended up in hospital, having been given a cocktail of drugs in her champagne, and had second-degree burns down her throat because the mixture contained a floor cleaner. She had to eat baby food for two months afterwards. Watch your drink, all the time, and don't trust people you don't know well not to give you something you don't want.

It may all sound scary but being aware of the risks will mean that you can minimise your chances of running into trouble. Always be alert and you'll be in a much better position to have pleasurable brief encounters. And that's what you're aiming for, after all.

Location, location, location

You won't find anyone to play with by staying in the house, unless you get lucky with the postie or the pizza delivery-man, and that happens way less than porn movies would suggest. Sadly, there's no 'single man storage unit' where you can go to pick up a nice-looking specimen to take home. However, getting out and about will increase your chances of meeting new people and, thus, getting laid.

Always scout for opportunities; you could pull outside the supermarket, or while waiting for a bus, or while you're wait-ing to be served in a shop, as well as in more obvious places such as down the pub with your mates. Certain places are particularly perfect for pulling, though, so here's a rough guide to finding your bit of rough (or, indeed, slick city gent).

Working girl

Nowadays, women spend more time than ever at work, so it's hardly surprising that a third of women have copped off with someone they met in the office. You've got an excuse to talk to a potential conquest, have some areas of common ground — even if it's just how much you both hate the boss — and may well end up socialising together after work, so opportunity is rife.

However, before you leap on Gary from Marketing, check your work policies on office lust. Some companies don't approve, particularly if a woman cops off with her boss. And if you're the boss and crave a night of fiery sex with someone junior to you, be aware that women can get charged with sexual harassment, too.

Assuming that you're allowed to go for it (or you fancy a taste of the forbidden) it's relatively easy to get a shag out of someone you work with. Go to the office parties, drop by the bar after work or indulge in flirting over the photocopier. You'll soon find out whether your office boy is game. If he's not, back off. You don't want him to have to deal with a stalker in his own office.

If you have sex someone you work with, it's critical that you ensure that the person you pick is discreet. You don't want to walk past the sales floor to hear the entire team imitating the sounds you make when you come; and you don't want to get a reputation for being the office slut. Sex is all very well, but damaging your professional reputation because of what goes on between your thighs is short-sighted.

It's also particularly important to make sure that a workmate knows the score before you get it on. It's far less embarrassing to be up-front about wanting a casual encounter than to deal with an enamoured workmate. Few things are worse than having to face someone making puppy-dog eyes at you every day when all you wanted was a night of passion.

A very thorough interview: Elisa's story

I've always had a lot of luck getting sex through work; there was a time when I'd shagged someone at every company I'd ever worked at. My favourite was probably Martin, though, because it felt so naughty.

I was interviewing for a new job and, after the interview was over, I was invited to join my potential new colleagues down the pub. Keen to impress, I said yes. It rapidly became clear that the company offered a good social life; most of the people in the pub seemed to work at the company I was interviewing for and I got introduced to lots of new people.

Unfortunately, one really ugly bloke, Greg, took a shine to me. I had no idea how important he was, so smiled sweetly, but when he put his hand on my bum,

I made an excuse and dashed to the toilet. Coming out a safe five minutes later, I almost walked into Martin. He'd seemed really friendly when we'd been introduced earlier and, after apologising for almost knocking him over, I decided to confide in him about the slimeball who was chatting me up. He was sympathetic – apparently, Greg was like that with all the women in the office – and offered to look after me. I gratefully took him up on his offer.

It turned out that Martin worked in a different department to the one I'd interviewed for – although he knew the person who'd interviewed me quite well – so, when he started flirting, I thought it was safe enough to respond.

As the evening progressed, the pub thinned out, but Martin and I carried on chatting. I got a bit tipsy and, as a result, when it got to pub closing time, I asked him if I could come back to his place. He – more than willingly – agreed. When we got back to his, we had another glass of wine and soon started kissing. One thing led to another and we ended up in bed. I didn't actually have sex with him but we did everything else.

A week later, I got a letter saying that I'd got the job. On my first day, I made a point of collaring Martin to ask whether he'd told anyone. He hadn't, and we agreed that it was best for us not to mention it, or do it again, now that we were working together.

His will-power was as bad as mine. For the first month or so that I worked there, every time we ended up in the pub together after work, I'd go back to his place. It was only sex – neither of us wanted a relationship – and no one in the company knew that it was going on. We deliberately left ten minutes between leaving his place so that we never arrived at work together, and I got into the habit of putting a clean top in my bag to change into the next day, 'just in case'.

Things fizzled out after a while, but we remained friends and our extra-curricular activities never impacted on work; it was just a bit of fun. It would have been a bit embarrassing had anyone found out but it was easy enough to keep it quiet because we are both discreet. Even though I left the company several years ago, I still have fond memories of the time that I pulled at an interview.

Through friends

Another common way of meeting potential fucks is through friends. Most people tend to have overlapping social groups so, unless you're in a small clique that keeps entirely to itself, you'll have lots of scope to meet new people.

Try to arrange regular group events, to make it easier for new people to get introduced to your friendship circle. Horse racing, visiting a casino or going to a gallery are better options than going to the cinema, though. You need to have enough time to make conversation with the new people, and it'll annoy the people in the row behind you no end if you chat through a film.

If arranging a group event sounds like it requires too much organisation, suggest a simple pub gathering where you all bring one or two new people along. Despite the *Sex and the City* episode that had a 'bring an ex' party, it's far safer to stick to bringing male friends rather than people you've already slept with. Jealousy can spring up, even if you don't think that it will, and a friend is more important than a fuck. It's worth seeing if any of your mates have foxy brothers, too; but check that they're OK with you shagging their sibling before you get it on. Some people get freaked out by that kind of thing. The safest bet is bringing along workmates or boys who are lovely, but you just don't fancy.

You can tell a lot about someone by the kind of people they hang out with, so there's a better than average chance that you'll have something in common with a friend of a friend. There are even websites like friendster.com set up based on this principle; you put in your details, as do your friends, and you can see who all their other friends are – and find a potential date.

If you do shag a mate's friend, make sure that you don't put them in an awkward situation. As always, be honest with your conquest about your intentions. You don't want your poor mate to be caught in the middle, with her boy mate asking why her you haven't called.

Horse racing led to pulse-racing: Cheryl's story

One of my girlie mates invited me to go to the horse racing to celebrate her other half's birthday. I wasn't really thinking of pulling – I thought I knew everyone who'd be there – but thought it sounded like a giggle so decided to give it a go. When I turned up, I was surprised to see that there was a huge group of people; mostly couples but with a few single guys I'd never met before. We were all comparing race-cards and, soon, everyone was chatting like old friends.

I'd never been to the races before, but it rapidly transpired that I sucked at betting; I think it had something to do with me picking horses based on their names or the colour they wore rather than their form. As the races went on, the group started to split into people who'd won, and people who'd lost, the winners peeling off to go and watch the horses closer up because they were really getting into it. Soon, there was just me and one other guy sitting at the table, having given up on betting because we'd both lost every race. We started a surreal conversation about alternatives to horse racing – racing kittens, for example – and it turned out we had a similarly quirky sense of humour. As luck would have it, he also turned out to live nearer me than anyone else did, so we shared a taxi home.

When we got back, we carried on chatting and one thing led to another. Unfortunately, it turned out that we are far more compatible as friends than lovers; the sex was fine but neither of us were blown away by it enough to want to go for it again. We're still in regular contact, though; I've promised to set him up with my mates and he's offered the same in return, so it certainly wasn't a wasted evening.

Forget Norma no-mates –
you're Confident Carrie

If all your mates are out on dates – or you've moved somewhere new and don't know anyone – don't be scared to go out on your own. It may take all your courage (and a stiff gin) but as long as you can get home safely it's a great way to meet new people, because men are less intimidated about approaching a woman on her own than one surrounded by a group of giggling mates. Pick somewhere that it's easy to strike up conversation, such as a bookshop or a pub with big tables that everyone shares. Take or wear an item that can act as a conversation starter, whether it's a book or a stylish piece of jewellery.

You could go for the 'taking a pet' route, but make sure that it's a big dog if you do. Men who make conversation with you because you've got a small, fluffy pooch probably won't be interested in you or, indeed, any woman. Spending time out on your own will also help build your confidence, as you'll learn to enjoy your own company more. And the more confident you are, the more you pull, so it's an all-round winner.

Party, party, party

Sometimes they're work gatherings, sometimes they're mates' events and sometimes you just happen to be in the right place at the right time to get an invitation but, whatever the occasion, parties are great places to pull. There's usually an excuse to start up conversation, in the form of 'So how do you know the host?' There's alcohol involved. And you've probably got a mate or colleague somewhere in the vicinity that you can sound out about your potential prospect, so they can warn you if the guy's got a reputation for being crap in the sack or is so ugly that you must be wearing beer-goggles.

One of the best ways of getting invited to lots of parties is to hold lots of parties; your guests are likely to return the invitation. Always let people bring mates with them, too, as you'll get to meet new people that way. By hosting your own party, you're in a good position to pick from the best of the bunch of men. You've got a ready-made excuse to talk to any bloke there; just introduce yourself and ask who brought him, explaining you're the hostess. Best of all, if it's a house-party, you'll be near your bedroom so you haven't got far to drag your conquest.

Even rubbish parties can lend themselves to pulling opportunities. If you hate it, chances are someone else will be having a crap time, too. All you need to do is find that person, establish whether they're fit and, if they are, lure them away to make your own entertainment.

Pulling at a party: Tom's story

I was quite young, 16 or 17 I think, and with a modest amount of success with the ladies. Some light frottaging, one multi-month 'relationship' that rid me of my virginity, an older woman who swapped her patience and experience for my youthful vigour and enthusiasm and assorted sundry other sordid encounters. To be frank, nothing really memorable. Then there was a contrived series of events that led me to be somewhere in the country at a party that I didn't want to be at with some adults I barely knew. And a girl.

It was a hot sunny day and I was dressed inappropriately in dark jeans, Doc Martins, a white T-shirt and my favourite black, shapeless sweater. She was pretty (although not stunning); blonde haired, blue eyed and seemed fairly shy. I was stuck in that horrid teenage boy quandary of wanting to impresses anything with tits with inappropriate displays of machismo while trying to affect an air of studied nonchalance.

We wandered around outside. Conversation was attempted but the combination of shyness, lack of any practical social graces and my goddamned attempts at playing cool scuppered the few conversational gambits that we both tried. We ended up in a field about a hundred meters down the road, sprawled on the ground, not talking. It was warm and the isolation from being surrounded by corn stalks made the situation seem rather dreamy, like putting your head underwater when you're in the bath. I took my sweater off and she laid on it, resting her head on my stomach.

We must have been there for about 20 minutes before I started to to say something, probably incredibly banal. She turned to look at me and I immediately shut up, mid word. Then she rolled over and unzipped my fly, reached inside my boxers and gently started massaging my cock. I had the good sense to shut up and just let it happen. When it was hard enough to fulfil some mysterious private criteria, she bent her head down and put her lips over the tip and I realised I was about to get my first proper blowjob. Not the crap attempts meted out in some alley by the girls I'd known previously, which were little more than rewards, treats handed out for having the persistence to pay attention all night and remembering to say the right things at the right time. Those were crude, aggressive, sometimes painful (I later found out that one of the girls at school had read in a magazine that using your teeth 'gently' was erotic). This was warm, enclosing, soft and a thousand times more erotic.

I lay back and just went with it. I was a very passive participant, to the point where I still wonder if it was for my benefit or not, and lean slightly towards the negative. I have no idea how long I lasted. I barely moved during the whole thing, only briefly curling my toes inside my Docs at the final moment. She zipped me up again and rolled over, resuming her previous position of lying on her back with her head on my stomach. I rested my hand lightly on her shoulder and she didn't remove it but neither did I attempt to move it elsewhere. The same sudden sexual clarity told me to just keep silent and not to try the typical teenage headlong rush to cup the breast or attempt to reach down over her bellybutton.

Another age passed and I think I fell asleep, when she suddenly stood up and began brushing herself off, saying 'We ought to get back.' Just like that; no sense of anything in her tone, no regret, no happiness, no reference to what had just happened. I nodded and we started off down the road in silence. At one point I took hold of her hand and she didn't stop me but by the time we got back to the party I think one of us had let go again. We found the adults, muttered something about having gone for a walk and then grunted our goodbyes in typical teenage fashion and that was it. I never saw her again.

Dating events

Forget images of seedy bars with sad men in polyester suits. Modern dating events are far sexier; they're designed to appeal to a younger and funkier crowd, and the men there are far from desperate losers. If you feel nervous about what you might encounter, take a single girlie mate with you for moral support. That way, it becomes a bit of fun for the pair of you, which reduces the pressure to pull, and will help you relax.

No matter what kind of a man you're looking to pull, there's an event designed to cater for your taste. Some of the quirkier events include:

- *Speed-dating*: You get to have up to 30 three-minute dates with people, then pick all the ones you like the look of by ticking a box. If they also like the look of you then – bang! – you're matched up and can arrange a date at your leisure.
- *Slow-dating*: As above, but you get four minutes per 'date' (still pretty speedy, though – 'ba-a-ang!', maybe).
- *Dinner in the dark*: You have dinner with potential partners in pitch black, only seeing them towards the end of the night, when the lights go on, and everyone notices they're covered in soup. Just kidding. Darkness is sexy and thrilling and encourages you to focus on personality rather than just looks. I mean, you're not shallow, right? It also allows lots of scope for groping under the table (if you're brave enough to risk getting a slap from a stranger, or groping someone ugly, that is).
- *Lock and key parties*: Men are given keys and women locks. Each lock and key is allocated a number of matches and, every time a match is found, the 'couple' is entered into a prize draw to win holidays. So even if you don't get lucky in love, you could end up one step closer to a holiday fling.

On top of all the dating events, there are also some great flirting courses out there, which are ideal places to meet new people as well as get pulling advice; see flirtcoach.com for details.

A foreign affair

Holidays are a prime picking ground for casual encounters. You're generally somewhere sunny, which is good for the libido, and being away from home can give even the shyest woman enough courage to approach the Adonis by the pool. (NB: If a man's wearing speedos, just don't. He'll be crap in the sack, a boring conversationalist or both. Worst of all, he's more likely than most men to choose thong-style underwear and, frankly, a girl can do without that kind of traumatic image burned into her brain.)

It's particularly important to carry condoms with you when you go on holiday, as you can't guarantee the local area will have condoms to buy that have been reliably clinically tested and thus safe. Added to which, if you get tipsy, it's the kind of thing that you're more likely to forget about until you're in his hotel room and, (heaven forbid) if you don't have condoms on you, you might be tempted to fuck him without one. STIs are all too easy to catch on holiday, and not just in countries you may be wary about. According to herpes.com, 22 per cent of adult Americans have oral or genital herpes. Coming back from holiday with a plastic replica of the Statue of Liberty is bad enough; you don't want to add blistering bits into the equation.

Remember, holiday spirit can make even the roughest-looking bloke seem gorgeous; he's got a tan, and you've probably got a fair few cocktails inside you. Enjoy your holiday sex for what it is, but don't expect your man to seem anything like as adorable once the holiday is over; you're likely to end up disappointed.

Holiday Romeo was rank in reality: Ally's story

I met a guy on holiday and, through the haze of Sangria, he seemed like a real stunner. We had a bit of a fling and I arranged to meet him when I got back home. I eagerly anticipated his arrival but, when he turned up, I was appalled to find that he was hideous; badly dressed with a face that looked like a squashed-up pug-dog. Nonetheless, he'd travelled a long way to see me so I felt obliged to give the poor lad something.

After we did the business, he fell asleep and snored like a pig, of wart-hog proportions. It was appalling. I ended up creeping into my living room and sleeping on the (tiny, two-person) sofa, covered in a bath towel.

He came in the next morning and said 'What are you doing?' and I said, 'Well, you snored.' He proceeded not to speak to me all morning.

He was supposed to be staying with me all weekend, but I made an excuse about an unexpected family visit and kicked him out by lunchtime (whereupon I met another guy I was seeing and had a much better time).

I never heard from him again but, five years later, I was temping in an office for a week, went to use the photocopier and there he was. We recognised each other, panicked and totally ignored each other. Mature ... Not a story I'm particularly proud of, all in all.

Web of desire

If you really can't bring yourself to leave the house, there's always the internet. You've got email, instant messaging and online dating sites to play with, so get typing.

Email can be a valuable flirting tool; indeed, it's hard to imagine that only ten years ago it was something that few people used. While asking for someone's phone number can be a bit embarrassing, asking for their email address is less of an issue. If you're chatting someone up and mention an article or film, you can easily slip into the conversation, 'Actually, I can mail it to you. What's your address?' without it being painfully obvious that you're on the pull. From there, you can get chatting over email and easily suggest meeting up for a drink. As an added bonus, people tend to be much more honest over email than they are in person, so you can also find out about a bloke's kinks and quirks before you get him in the sack.

Enticing email: Belinda's story

The last three men I shagged all came through email. In Pete's case, we'd met through work a few years before. He emailed me out of the blue to ask about a project that he'd heard I was working on, and we soon descended into flirting. We'd both been attached when we knew each other, but had subsequently become single. We decided to meet up and there followed a couple of months of great sex.

While I was with Pete, I met a guy when I was out with a group of mates. We liked each other but I was doing the faithful thing, so didn't want to make a move on him. We got on well, though, so we swapped email addresses and ended up sending each other a chatty message most days. When I became single, I told him and we hooked up for a drink. I invited him back to my place afterwards and we shagged each other senseless. We decided that it was best keeping it as a one-off as neither of us was ready for a relationship, but carried on flirting vaguely over email.

Then came Max, a cute guy who I bumped into at a mutual friend's party one night. He was shy so I didn't want to give him a heavy come-on. Instead, I asked him for his business card and mailed him the next day to say how nice it had been meeting him. We emailed each other for about a month and, once I thought it wouldn't scare him off, I asked him out for a drink. We met up and, because we'd spent so long getting to know each other via email, he was relaxed enough to come back to my place with the minimum of persuasion.

Email is an essential part of pulling for me now. It's useful for getting to know people, and it's far less embarrassing getting rejected over email than over the phone – not that I've been rejected yet.

One word of warning about email: many work computers are vetted for content, so if you send anything too lewd then your object of desire may not get the mail. Sending pervy messages can also result in serious shame if the bloke forwards it to someone else, as Claire Swires found out five years ago. She sent her boyfriend a kinky message, which he forwarded to a friend. His friend also forwarded it on and, before long, it had been sent to half the world. While there are rumours of this story being a hoax, it illustrates a valid point; once you've clicked 'send', you don't know what the person receiving a message will do with it so, unless you really trust a guy, don't get too rude.

Instant messaging (IM) via computer is another handy pulling tool. You can use it in a similar way to email; ask a potential conquest if he uses instant messaging and, if so, get to know him over IM before moving in for the kill. Or you can use it to pull strangers; just fire up your computer and start searching the chat-rooms. A quick search in your preferred search engine (eg Yahoo!) will soon return some saucy options.

Many instant messaging programmes (AIM, MSN or whatever) include chat-rooms of all flavours. Be prepared for a glut of people asking A/S/L? (age/sex/location) and some conversation that makes Woody Woodpecker seem eloquent but, with a bit of patience, you can wade through the dross to find someone worth getting your rocks off with.

Whether you're chatting one-to-one or having fun in a chat-room, just let your fingers do the talking. If you're talking to a stranger, don't give away any personal details, such as your real name, address, email address or where you work, and be sure to use a username that doesn't give any identifying information (though, given the amount of 'Big-Boobs' out there, you're probably safe picking something like that). Other than that, you're free to say or do whatever you feel like, so indulge your imagination to the full.

Not only is IM useful for pulling but, if you're feeling frisky but can't be bothered with getting dressed up and making a full-on effort to pull, just switch on that computer and there are a wealth of men (and women) out there who are all too willing to talk filth with you. While it may not be quite as much fun as skin-to-skin contact, it's certainly safer, and is a good way to explore your fantasies. If you add a webcam to the equation, you can get naked with your online lover, to add an extra frisson. However, if you do go for it, make sure that your head isn't visible. You probably won't want pictures of you indulging in perviness being posted on porn sites.

Internet addict: Katie's story

I went through a phase of having cybersex almost every night, all of it with people I knew, at least over email. Some of the cybersex ended up translating into offline sex; after all, I knew what the guys wanted in bed, because they'd told me, and had an idea of what they'd be like too (in some cases, I even knew how big they were because we often used webcams). Other cybersex stayed purely virtual; there was one guy who was amazing at tapping into my submissive fantasies but there was no way that I'd have wanted to do the stuff we discussed in real life.

I gave it up after about a year, because I realised that I was getting hooked on it; I'd race back from evenings out because I wanted to have cybersex with someone who I knew would be online. Needless to say, it wasn't exactly helping my 'real life' pulling chances.

Looking back, I'm a bit embarrassed about it all; telling mates of mine all the intimate thoughts that I had but, at the time, I enjoyed it. It's far too easy to get hooked though – and the real thing is much better.

Online dating has way less of a stigma attached than it used to; a Bath University study found that a third of internet users have tried it and, according to datingdirect.com, 68 per cent of people think online dating is better than its offline equivalent. Websites can get rid of some of the selection legwork too; there are sites out there for vegetarians, graduates, every ethnic group, 'fat' people, 30+s, 'gorgeous' people and pretty much any other category you can imagine. Several sites are designed specifically for people who are after casual encounters or who want to live out a particular fantasy. So no matter what kind of man you're after, you should find him online.

You can up your pulling chances online by investing in some decent pictures of yourself. Female photographer Nahid de Belgeonne runs sauce-goddess.co.uk and specialises in taking classy erotic pics that make any woman look gorgeous. Forget those Vaseline-tinted lens monstrosities; she chats to women to find out what they're like and how they want to look, then helps them show off their ultimate assets in her pictures. But even though Nahid can take nude pics, it's better to pick one of the more innocent shots unless you're happy with the idea of strangers using them as free porn; either that or crop any pictures so that they only show your head and shoulders.

It's also worth bringing a bit of psychology into play when you write your advert. According to Professor Robin Dunbar of Liverpool University, men look for (in order): attractiveness, commitment, social skills, resources and sexiness. However, if you're writing an advert to appeal to a bi babe, the order changes. Women go for commitment, social skills, resources, attractiveness and then sexiness – although lesbians are three times less likely to seek resources than heterosexual women.

So having posted your pic and written your ad designed with maximum pulling power in mind, just wait for your inbox to be filled with tempting offers. However, you should make sure that you keep yourself safe when meeting someone in person who you've first 'met' online. Don't give out your home address or phone

Dealing with 'I'm not fabulous' moments

No matter how confident you are, at some stage you're bound to have moments when you feel less than fabulous. If you're indulging in brief encounters, this is more than likely to happen on a Saturday night, when you're convinced the rest of the world is out having hot dates that will lead to steamy encounters and you're sitting at home, realising that Saturday night TV is rubbish and wishing that you'd got round to getting a video membership card.

This is normal. Chances are there's some woman sitting four doors down from you feeling exactly the same way, and wishing she'd never dumped her ex, even though he farted and held her head under the duvet.

As with casual sex, lonely nights in are worth preparing for. So, here's your essential list to ensure you never have a really crap night in again:

- *A bottle of champagne:* While alcohol isn't the answer, there's only so depressed that it's possible to be when you have bubbly in the house. If you can't afford a cheap bottle of champagne then get a decent sparkling wine at about half the price. Keep it chilled and, if you're feeling rubbish because you're spending a night in alone, flip the finger at solitude and pour yourself a glass. The bubbles should fill you with frivolity. (NB: Don't drink the entire bottle — fizz will keep perfectly well for at least a night as long as you keep it cold — otherwise you'll get all maudlin and call your idiot ex.)

- *Posh bubble bath*: This needn't cost a fortune. Go round department store cosmetics counters in your most expensive clothes and explain that you have sensitive skin but their products come highly recommended, so could you have a sample to try. Most of the time this works a dream and you'll go back laden with freebies. And ask your girlie mates to buy you bath things for your birthday. Reclining in a bubbly bath will help you feel much more chilled out. And you can guarantee that attached mates won't have the luxury; they'll have to deal with a bloke bashing on the door desperate to get in and use the facilities.

- *Gorgeous nightwear*: Reclining in front of the TV or listening to music while wearing a gorgeous silk night-dress or snuggly pair of flannelette pyjamas will help you feel like spending a night in is your choice. Which, of course, it is. If you're gagging for a shag, you could always go to your local and accept offers from some drunk. You've just decided to spend a night in, indulging in 'quality time'. No, really, you *have*.

- *Something to cuddle*: Sometimes, all you need to cheer you up is a big hug, and there are few things worse than having no one to hug you. If you don't have a male friend who can provide the required snuggling, the next best thing is a furry animal (why do you think so many single women have cats?). If the idea of looking after a pet fills you with horror, the next best thing is a fake cat that really purrs (available from firebox.com). You can hug it all night and its fur can be cried into.

- *A good book*: Forget self-help books (except this one, obviously). Instead, go for a trashy novel or your favourite high-brow author. Before you know it, you'll be so immersed in the lives of the characters that you'll have forgotten all about being in on your own.

If all else fails, and you're still feeling lonely, go for the cybersex option. It's always there and you can guarantee there will be someone out there who's desperate to hear from a babe like you.

number, pick a neutral location and arrange for a friend to call you half an hour into the date to make sure that you're OK. Having fun doesn't mean taking unnecessary risks, even if you are just meeting up for casual sex.

The most important thing to remember is that pulling opportunities are everywhere and, the more you get out, the higher your chance of getting a guy in the sack. Read local listings and see what's going on. Maybe there's an exhibition you'd like to see or a new restaurant opening? Go to places that reflect your interests and you're more likely to meet someone who you can make conversation with – which is the first step towards getting someone in the sack.

Talking the talk: chat-up tricks that really work

Chat-up lines have a bad reputation, and rightly so. People are different, so using the same line on everyone just won't work. However, women can get away with lines way easier than men. A lot of the time, a man will be so flattered that you've approached him that you can say 'Do you come here often?' and he'll think you're a sparkling raconteur.

Psychologists claim a whopping 38 per cent of communication is down to your tone of voice. Keep it friendly and low for maximum desirability. Talk quietly and a man will have to come closer to hear you. And if you end up whispering in his ear, the feeling of your breath may well get him begging for a private conversation.

Having confidence is also important. That's why you can go to a party wearing your most stylish designer outfit, only to spend most of the night alone because you aren't feeling confident; or, conversely, nip out to the shops in your 'lounging around' clothes and pull the gorgeous guy in front of you in the queue. When you're not looking for sex, you're more likely to act naturally. And if you look confident, you look like you'll be a fun person to spend time with, so you're more likely to get laid.

What not to say: Lisa's story

Both my brothers were at a party years ago in London. My youngest brother, Jake, met an Australian girl and things started heating up. She then said in her broad Aussie accent, 'Gee mate, I'm ridin' the rag at the moment but you can do it up me shitter if ya like'. Funnily enough Jake changed his mind.

Almost everyone gets nervous when they first approach someone they're interested in, so sometimes it can seem easier to have a 'line' to fall back on. You're more likely to get a positive response if you're honest (OK, not too honest; saying, 'I've just been picturing you smothered in ice-cream,' will probably scare most men off but there's nothing wrong with letting someone know you think they're a fox).

Most people have got at least one horror story about chat-up lines. Maybe you've been asked, 'Are your legs tired? You've been running through my mind all day.' (To which the only suitable response is, 'Yes, I was looking for a brain cell.') Or perhaps you've been the person cringing when someone gives you change and tells you to call your mum because you're not going home. Either way, chat-up lines only work if the person concerned is already interested. Otherwise, you're just as likely to get a withering look as a fuck.

If possible, get a mutual friend to introduce you, picking their brains about your target's interests first. Opening a conversation with, 'So I hear you're ace at rock-climbing – I was thinking of going on a course. Have you got any tips?' will make a man feel all masterful and he'll willingly seize the opportunity to show you how informed he is.

If the person is a stranger, stand near him and subtly listen in on the conversation. When something comes up that you know about, lean over, smile and say, 'I couldn't help overhearing, and I had to say that I agree with what you're saying. Have you heard … ?' or something similar. By showing you're on-side with his argument, you'll be demonstrating that you're clearly a woman he should get to know better. With any luck you'll get integrated into the conversation and can get to know your object of desire and decide whether he's worthy to share your bed.

If your potential conquest is alone, try to pick up on a shared interest. Ask open-ended questions to make the conversation easy. Clothes can give you an indication of what to ask. Perhaps he's got that surf look going on or is a city suit type. Maybe he's carrying a record bag branded for a particular band. If he's reading, comment on the book (apologising for interrupting first). If you're in a bar, buy a drink when he does and see if you can start a conversation based on what he buys; ask him to recommend a wine or whether his beer is OK because the last one you had here was a bit iffy.

Asking a potential conquest about himself is flattering as it shows that you are interested in him. Also, almost every man enjoys talking about himself. It makes him feel interesting, valued and, quite simply, happy – and it's no bad thing at all for your chances if a guy feels that he's happier since he started talking to you. Laugh at a bloke's jokes too. Men love this – it makes them feel all big and clever, which is always a good way to get them on-side. A shared sense of humour is a great way to bond – you can literally laugh someone into bed.

Avoid the question, 'What do you do?' It may seem like you're more interested in his wallet than his personality, or he could have a job that he's embarrassed about. Ask him what he enjoys doing instead. By finding out a man's interests early on, it also means you can avoid guys who are avid readers of *Serial Killers Monthly* or find nothing more scintillating than spending a Saturday afternoon searching for a new stamp for their collection.

One killer line that almost always works is simply telling a man you enjoy his company. Say something along the lines of, 'I'm having a great time with you. Can we go out sometime to chat more?' to get the message across without putting yourself on the line. If you don't ask, you won't get anywhere. If you *do* ask, you've got a chance of getting the person of your erotic dreams.

Brazen hussy: Anna's story

I'd fancied Ben for ages and every time we saw each other we flirted with each other but, to my disappointment, things never seemed to progress. After six months, I decided that enough was enough; it had got to the stage where the flirting was closer to talking dirty, and I wanted to know where I stood.

I found out that Ben was going to be at a networking event I was going to, so I got dressed up in my favourite outfit and spent an age getting my make-up just right. When I arrived, he wasn't there. I was nervous, so I had one too many gin and tonics to give myself Dutch courage.

After about three hours, he turned up. I was hammered, so I had no qualms about approaching him. The alcohol had turned off any degree of subtlety I'd had, though. I stumbled up to him and drawled (possibly drooled), 'We've been flirting for ages but what I've got to know is … do you fancy a fuck or what?' He was horrified. He mumbled, 'Err, yes, err, no, err, I don't know,' before making an excuse and escaping as soon as he could. It was humiliating beyond belief. Now, if I fancy someone, I'll still let them know – but I'd never be that obvious again.

Let your body do the talking

So, you've got the words to work your magic, but that's only one part of the story. Body language accounts for at least 55 per cent of communication, and the clues that your body gives away can be even more important than what you say. After all, how many times have you been attracted to a guy just because there's 'something' about him? It's partly down to body chemistry, but it's got a lot to do with body language.

Understanding what your body is saying will help you use it to maximum advantage. Relax in front of the mirror and look at your natural posture. Train yourself to make it 'open', with your hands unclenched and arms at your sides. You want to look like you're sexy, fun and available. In body language, this means avoiding 'closed' postures. Don't fold your arms or cross your legs as it puts up a barrier between you and your object of desire.

Body language comes in particularly handy when you're at a noisy bar or the local club, where you can't hear a word anyone's saying. Not only can you use non-verbal clues to let a bloke know you want to jump his bones, but you can also spot whether a man's hot to trot with you.

What he'll do – and how to respond

If a bloke's interested he will:
- Face you with his head tilted;
- Have his hands behind his head, touching his arms;
- Lean forwards;
- Talk animatedly;
- Make lots of eye contact;
- 'Echo' your body posture.

Show your interest by:
- Tilting your head to one side, facing slightly away from your conquest;
- Keeping your arms – but not your legs – open;
- Flicking your hair;
- Touching your body, stroking your collarbone or neck, or putting your hands on your hips;
- Leaning your body slightly backwards;
- Repeatedly crossing and uncrossing your legs.

Sneaky tricks to look more appealing

If you use every inch of your body to make him desperate for more, you'll be blown away by the results.

Hairs and graces: There's a reason why flirtatious women are depicted twirling their hair; 'grooming' behaviour demonstrates interest. (Be careful if you wear a lot of hair-styling products; it's not exactly sexy if you get your hand stuck in a cluster of hair-sprayed locks.)

Eye want you: Eye contact is vital. Don't stare. Just look into your target's eyes for fractionally longer than usual, look away, then glance back. If he's looking back, you're probably in.

Hanging out where it's dark will make your pupils dilate, which makes you appear more attractive because it suggests arousal (it's one of the reasons that candlelight is so flattering). Courtesans used to put drops of belladonna (Deadly Nightshade) in their eyes to dilate their pupils but, as the name suggests, it's highly poisonous, so that's one trick best left in history.

It's worth thinking pervy thoughts when you're chatting someone up too, as this also makes your pupils dilate. Of course, if you fancy a bloke, it shouldn't be that difficult to think sexy thoughts; just imagine what you'll be doing to him later.

If you end up blushing, don't worry, as flushed skin is another turn on. Your skin flushes when you have an orgasm so it sends subliminal sex messages into a man's head.

Lip tricks: You already know how important your lips are when it comes to attracting a guy, but it's not just the right lipstick that can tempt a man to kiss you. Moisten your lips with your tongue when speaking to

Turning down grim blokes with grace

If you're out and about doing the pulling thing, chances are there will be blokes out to pull you, too. While some of them may be adorable, others would make shagging a cactus appealing by comparison, so you need to have escape routes.

The obvious line would seem to be 'You're not my type,' but that line is not only hard to say for a lot of women – we don't like upsetting people, after all – but also rarely works. It just makes men get annoyed, which is no fun at all. Saying you're a lesbian may sound like a plan, but it will never work on a drunk man; he'll either assuming you're lying or pester you all night to watch.

The ultimate trick is to always wear a ring on your engagement finger. Most men will accept the 'My fiancé wouldn't like it' rejection, whereas 'I've got a boyfriend' rarely works. Sure, one or two men may notice it and be put off, but anyone interested will ask.

someone you fancy; wet lips are a natural turn on for men, and glimpses of tongue can be intimate, too. He'll start imagining where else it could lick. Make sure you've got lipbalm on you, particularly in winter; scabby lips are far from sexy.

Smile a lot, glancing at areas of your prospect's body without focusing on any intimate parts. Not only will it make you seem more approachable, it's also good for you, producing endorphins that boost your mood. You may smile because you're happy, but the act of smiling will make you even happier, and happy women get laid more often. Then again, that could be why they're happy.

Get into his zone: Nod your head when chatting to a guy you fancy and use hand gestures to bring him into your conversation. The aim here is to make him feel included, like it's just you and him in a private world. You can also try this over a table: move your arm into 'his space' (his half of the table). If he leans back then you're invading his space; if he leans forward, he doesn't object at all. From there, it's just one small step into bed.

Touching a bloke up will also get him interested — but don't go for his knob. Make small touching movements, lightly placing your fingers on 'safe' areas of his body — his shoulders, arms and wrists. The old 'You've got some fluff on you' is a good excuse. Feeling your fingers on his body will make a man wonder what it would be like to be touched elsewhere.

Mirroring: Copying a man's movements will attract him. If he crosses his arms, you should cross yours. If he leans back, do the same. If he touches your arm, wait a little while then return the gesture. This suggests on a subconscious level that you are similar people. Be careful about taking this too far; if he wanders off to go to the toilet, you'll just seem 'scary stalker' if you follow him.

Chapter 5

How to Be the Best Lover Ever

If you've followed the guidelines and all's gone to plan, by now you should have someone to join you for a night of hot love action. But what now? Obviously, you know roughly what you want out of your man – namely, some hot sex – but first you need to get over that uncomfortable 'We both know what you're here for but who's going to pounce?' moment. It's all too easy to fall into the trap of waiting for him to make the first move, while he's waiting for you to do the same thing. The next thing you know, it's morning and neither of you have had any (or worse, he's made his excuses and left, figuring that he misread the signals).

Even once that first move is out of the way, it's not all plain sailing. Your man may be a crap kisser, or you might be terrified by the size of his truncheon when you unleash it (or have to get out a magnifying glass just to see it). Never fear. As boring manager types are inclined to say, 'There are no problems, only solutions'. And no matter what happens between the sheets, you can guarantee some poor woman has been there before.

There's no need to be pessimistic about things. In most cases, you can have a raunchy night together without anything calamitous happening and, with a few nifty moves, you can turn it into the night of your life. If you like the idea of being the ultimate love-goddess – and let's face it, what woman doesn't – then learning a few tricks will mean that your man leaves your flat in the morning with a new-found faith in God (and distinctly wobbly knees). If you're really lucky, he might even tell his mates how incredible you were, and you'll get a queue of men desperate to sample your prodigious talents.

Making the move

Regardless of what the magazines might say, men still like making the first move, but they're often clueless when it comes to knowing when the time is right. And who can blame them? With the amount of date rape out there, a nice guy will be wary about doing anything you don't like. So you need to make it so screamingly obvious that you're hot to trot with him that he doesn't feel shy about going for it.

Women are impossible to read: Jonathan's story

I've lost count of the amount of women I've met who've told me, years later, that when we first met they really fancied me. The only problem is that none of them ever said so at the time. One woman expected me to pick up on her playing a sexy song when we were at her house. Another one asked me round for dinner but, when I turned up, one of her mates was there so I figured she just saw me as a friend (it turned out she wanted her mate's opinion of me). The gutting thing is that I fancied the women concerned and would have gone for it if I'd only realised that they were interested.

Depending on how brave – or brazen – you are, you could just be up-front about it and tell the man that you'd be happy for him to make a move, but it's hardly up there in classy seduction techniques. It's far better to let your body do the talking. You already know the basics of body language but now's the time to pull out the heavy artillery.

It may sound obvious, but make sure that you're close enough to your man for him to make a lunge. There's no point sitting on an armchair while he's on the sofa; he'll have to walk over the room to leap on you and that's going to be as intimidating as hell for him. Sit next to him on the sofa or, if you only have chairs, either pull them closer together or sit on a cushion at his feet (you can always use

How to turn a crap kisser into a good one

As Cher so rightly sang, 'It's in his kiss' and, as a general guide, if there's no chemistry when you kiss a bloke, you're probably heading for a disappointing shag. That said, sometimes you can feel sparks with someone but still find their technique somewhat lacking. Luckily, it's easy to fix.

If he's got bad breath, you should notice before you get to the snogging stage, so have a piece of chewing gum and offer him one. With any luck, he'll take it and the problem will go away. Of course, a bloke who goes out on the pull with bad breath may well be a thoughtless lover, so think carefully before you take things further.

If he's lunging at you as if he's trying to swallow you whole rather than kiss you, put your hands on either side of his head to pull him back. You can always pretend that your firm grip is passion-induced. Go for gentle kisses on his lips to slow things down.

If he thrusts his tongue too hard into your mouth, pull away and say something like, 'Mmmm, let's go gently. I'll show you what gets me really horny,' and deliver the perfect soft kiss. He should get the message and calm his pace.

If, on the other hand, he's not passionate enough, try very gently nibbling his lip to suggest you want the heat to rise, or pull back and say, jokingly, 'Kiss me like you mean it'. This may lead to more problems as you collapse into giggles at coming out with such a porntastic phrase but, if you can keep a straight face, it should do the trick.

If he's too wet a kisser, pull away and kiss his neck or shoulder to mop up the moisture before returning to kiss him. (NB: One woman I know swears that wet kissers tend to turn bunny-boiler so should be kicked out at the earliest opportunity.)

If you still can't get a decent kiss out of him, you have two choices. Give up and kick him out, or prepare yourself for a lacklustre shag. If he can't read your signals well enough to kiss you the way you most like it, he won't have a hope in hell of reading sex signals.

the excuse of being near the ashtray/bottle of wine so that you don't look like some subservient romantic).

If you're sitting next to a man on the sofa, leaning across his body — say, to get the remote control for the stereo — will make it easier for him to see you're interested, particularly if you move slowly and make eye contact when you're near his face. From there, he should go for the kiss.

If that doesn't work, the eye-to-lip glance has a scary rate of success. First, make eye contact. Leisurely drop your gaze to your object of desire's lips, then return to his eyes. Repeat this. By the third time you look at his lips, he'll be drawn to kiss you.

My mouth was full of blood: Angela's story

I'd always thought that kissing was a pretty safe activity to indulge in but Tim proved me wrong. I pulled him at the student club night and we were kissing up against a wall on my way home. I didn't really like the way he kissed – it was really aggressive – but I thought it was just because he was turned on, so decided not to say anything.

Then he started sucking my tongue. Hard. Even writing the next bit makes me feel nauseous. I heard a pop and felt my mouth fill with blood. He sucked so hard that he broke the stringy bit on the underside of my tongue.

It all happened so quickly that he didn't realise what he'd done. I pushed him away and, when he saw me spitting blood onto the floor, he looked confused. After the pain had faded, I told him the problem in no uncertain terms and stormed off on my own. There was no way that I was letting him get any further if he could draw blood just from kissing me.

Another good way of initiating physical contact without actually making a move is to rub your shoulders, in a 'God, I'm achy' way and ask if he'd mind giving you a massage. Not only will this be an end in itself, but it also shows him that you like the idea of his hands on your body. If he can't pick up on a signal that strong, you're dealing with an utterly clueless boy.

Honesty about STIs

It is absolutely vital to be open and honest with your sexual partner or partners if you have a Sexually Transmitted Infection (STI). Coyness or embarrassment is no excuse. You should tell the truth to everyone you want to shag, well before clothes have parted from flesh. If someone won't shag you because you have an STI, sorry, but you have to respect their decision. It's their health and their choice to make.

If you've tried everything else to no avail but are sure he fancies you (and if he's come back to your place, he almost definitely does), then you can make the first move. There are various approaches that can work. If he says something self-deprecating, go with the 'Aww, that's so sweet. Give me a hug,' line. It's then easy to move from the hug to a kiss.

Alternatively, go for another 'softly, softly' approach; let your hand casually rest against his thigh when you're sitting next to him, then slowly start stroking him in a vague way, as if it's unconscious. As he responds, move to more obvious stroking and either lean over to kiss him, or look into his eyes and he'll hopefully pick up on the hint and kiss you.

Of course, you might want things to move somewhat faster. If so, you can pin him to the wall as soon as you get inside the flat and have a rampant snogging session, with clothes flying in all directions.

For a slower approach – that cuts out any need for foreplay at all – put on a porn video. He'll get the horn, as will you (probably) and soon you'll be immersed in your own live action version of what's happening on screen.

If you're really brave – and know for certain that he's interested –just go out of the room and come back naked. It's not subtle but it will let him know you're interested in no uncertain terms.

From sofa to sack

Now that things are getting physical, it's a good time to bring up that condom question, ideally before you move to fondling each other. If you've agreed that you're using a condom in advance, it saves embarrassment spoiling the mood when things are getting hot. Added to which, if you've forgotten your condoms and he doesn't have any in the house, the last thing you want is to have to get dressed again for a walk to the nearest shop or bar.

You may feel embarrassed or think that talking about condoms will make the man feel like you're accusing him of having a disease, or label you as a trollop. Nowadays, that shouldn't be the case. Safer sex is the responsible thing to do and no good man should expect anything less. If he refuses to wear a condom, don't put out. After all, that probably means that he's refused to use condoms with partners before and is thus even more of a health risk.

Once you've dealt with the issue of condoms, you've just got to deal with the logistics of moving from sofa to the sack. This will probably happen naturally – you'll be falling off the sofa from too much groping and one of you will suggest moving somewhere more comfortable.

You might just decide to do it right there and then. Make sure that you don't stain the cushions; they're a pig to clean, unless you've got washable slip-covers, and you don't want everyone else to see the evidence of your conquests. Other hazards to watch out for are carpet-burn, which can take an age to get better and really limits the positions you can shag in; candles that can be all too easily knocked over in the heat of passion; and flatmates wandering in unannounced. On the plus side, if you know you want to kick a bloke out as soon as he's done his duty, it's a lot easier to get rid of him from the floor than from your bed.

Dealing with his excuses

Some blokes have an objection to wearing condoms, claiming that it ruins the experience for them. There may be a small degree of truth in this, but it won't ruin the sensation as much as catching an STI will, so protect yourself – and him – by countering his pathetic excuses with one of these lines:

- But I don't get any sensation if I wear a condom.
  You'll get way more sensation than you will if you don't get any sex. I'll put a little lube inside the condom if you want.
- Condoms are too tight on me.
  It's OK. I've got some Trojan Magnums, which are designed for big boys like you.
- I haven't had sex for ages so I can't have anything.
  I'm pretty sure I'm clean too but not everything's got symptoms, so you can't guarantee that – let's play it safe.
  or
  I'm not on the pill.
- I thought you liked me but you can't or you wouldn't ask me to wear one.
  And if you liked me you wouldn't expect me to put myself at risk.

- It will ruin the mood if I have to stop to put it on.

  Not if I help you ...
- It's a special occasion – just this once?

  Once is enough to catch something horrid.
- I haven't got any condoms.

  That's OK, I have.

  or

  OK, we can just fool around then.

  or

  We can go to get some together.
- I've had a vasectomy so it's safe.

  But you don't know where I've been.
- I don't want to ruin the intimacy.

  It'll feel a lot more intimate if we both know we're safe.
- Do I look like the kind of person who'd have a disease?

  We both know you're gorgeous but it's best for us both to be safe.
- My religion says that using condoms is wrong.

  It probably thinks casual sex is wrong then.
- You must be a slut if you want to use condoms.

  No — I respect myself and am trying to keep us safe (rapidly followed by ordering a taxi to get away from the idiot who said it).

In all other cases, bed is the optimum choice for sex. It's comfortable and designed for the purpose (well, and sleeping) after all. You can guarantee that if you get up and head to the bedroom, he'll follow you, but if you want to make really sure, lead him by the hand 'seductress-style'. With any luck, you'll both be so horny by now that it won't ruin the mood one iota.

Making the most of making out

Now you're in the bedroom, things will start heating up rapidly. What you get up to is entirely down to you, but you need to make sure that he knows what you want – and you know what he wants.

Even the most eloquent man can turn Neanderthal when it comes to communicating about sex, so you'll probably need to take the lead. When you touch him, ask if he likes it, and whether he'd prefer you stroking, licking or whatever. If you start to get tired with one activity, move on to another: men have tonnes of erogenous zones so you've got lots to play with.

Hand-jobs without wrist-ache

We've all been there; pumping away at some bloke who's stubbornly refusing to come, feeling the lactic acid build up and wondering if the wrist-ache will ever go away. But there's no need for pain when delivering the perfect hand-job. No matter how long a man takes to come, using the right technique will mean that you'll have the staying power to handle it.

First off, use lube. It will make the skin slip under your fingers much more easily, reducing friction and the amount of effort it takes to wank him.

One really simple lube technique is to slather his cock in the stuff and then, rather than moving your hand up and down, simply tighten and loosen your grip. The lube means that his cock will slide between your fingers of its own volition, with far less effort for you than an up/down motion takes.

One of the most common complaints that men have about women's hand-jobs is that they're too gentle, so get a good grip. Imagine you're delivering a firm handshake (though don't picture this too vividly or it could lead to embarrassment at your next business meeting).

Two hands can be better than one, in energy-saving terms as well as sensation for him. Entwine your fingers, then, sitting between his legs and facing him, move your hands up and down. You can also use the same grip technique as with one hand to save yet more energy.

You can also use tricks to help speed along his orgasm. Ask him how much pressure he likes, or even get him to show you what to do. Most men can make themselves come pretty damned quickly – and practise regularly – so he's bound to have a few techniques up his sleeve. Slipping a well-lubed finger up his anus works for some men, but check first. Caressing the balls or stroking the perineum can also help speed his climax.

How to escape if you change your mind

While sex is all very lovely, sometimes you can get back to a bloke's place and realise that, frankly, you don't want to cop off with him. It could be before things get heated; he mentions that he's always fancied your mum and you realise he's not the man for you. It could be after you've snogged him and realise that, despite your best efforts, there's no chemistry. Or it could be once you've got naked. Whatever stage it happens at, remember *you don't need to go through with it*. He might be a bit pissed off, but that's better than you hating every second that you're shagging, or feeling rubbish in the morning.

If it's relatively early on in proceedings, either invent an early meeting you'd forgotten all about or fake receiving a text message from a mate in trouble and say you have to go. Alternatively, burst into tears and say 'I just can't do this. I still love [insert name here]'. Most men are a tad uncomfortable with handling crying women and he'll be pushing you out the door.

If you're naked, the first thing to do is get your kit back on. This is done most easily by nipping off to the bathroom, picking your clothes up en-route. Then, when you return, fully clothed, you can use the 'friend in trouble' or 'early meeting' lines. Remember, no always means no, even if he says that you've 'led him on'. Having a shag because it's easier than refusing is only going to make you feel bad.

If he tries forcing the issue, get out as quickly as you can. You never know when someone is going to 'turn' and it's better to be safe than sorry. And if (heaven forbid) he tries to pin you down, one thing that may help is if you slide your legs inside his (assuming you're missionary style) then spread your legs as wide as you can. Men's hips are less flexible than women's and it will rapidly become painful for him, and can even damage his calf muscles. While he's in agony, run like hell. Forget about gathering up your belongings. You can always get to the nearest police station and get them to collect them for you.

It's not meant to scare you, but being aware of the risks and knowing how to escape will help you prevent getting into nasty situations. Brief encounters are about having fun, not having sex whether you want to or not.

Don't underestimate the visual element either. After all, often, when a man masturbates, he'll use some form of porn to help speed him along. So give him something to look at while you wank him. Spread your legs, or even use a toy with one hand while you stroke him with the other. You'll be surprised at how much it can speed things along. And, unlike blow-jobs, when you're wanking a guy your mouth isn't full so use it for talking dirty. Some people get a bit embarrassed at the idea of sex talk but there's no need to. A few phrases at the right moment can get your partner firing on all cylinders. Keep it simple at first and soon steamy talk will come naturally. Tell him how gorgeous his cock is, ask him if he likes you stroking him or let whatever filth that enters your head come out of your mouth.

If you get really shattered while giving a hand-job, you have various options. Ask him to put his hand over yours and set the pace (though some men can grip your hand too hard, so take off any rings first or they'll dig in uncomfortably).

Ask him to take over entirely; if you want to give him a real treat, ask him to wank over your tits – it's the kind of porn move that men are easily impressed by, and you get to lie back and have a rest. Or move on to blowing him, remembering to put that flavoured condom on first, of course. Loads of STIs can be transmitted through oral sex, so it's better to be safe than sorry. It should go without saying but, if you have a cold sore, don't even think of blowing him (or kissing him). You could give him herpes, which is the last thing that he'll want from his casual encounter.

Blow him away: giving the perfect blow job

Man 1: *Describe the worst blow job you've ever had.*
Man 2: *Pretty damn good!*

It may be an old joke but, to a large extent, it's true. As long as you don't bite, blow or generally damage his bits then your man will probably love it. However, there are a few things you can do to make it better.

Lots of men like the power kick that comes from being fellated by a woman who's on her knees, and love the way it looks, too. However, if this sets your feminist hackles rising, get him to lie on his back and then kneel between his legs. This angle means that you can get him far enough down your throat for it to be incredibly enjoyable for him, gives him a great view but also puts you in control. Try looking into his eyes while you 'perform' to give him a sexy thrill.

Use your hands as well as your mouth when you're performing oral sex. Put your hand around his shaft and your lips around the head of his penis then move your hand and mouth up and down in time with each other, licking and sucking as you go.

If you have long hair, try stroking it across his balls while you suck him. Some men put their hands on the back of your head when you're performing. It makes it far harder for you to stay in control and keep things comfortable, so indicate that you don't want him to do it if this is the case.

Unfortunately, some guys just aren't clean down there. If he's one, suggest a shower beforehand so he smells sweet and tastes good. Or keep a flannel by the side of the bed; that way, you can give him a bed-bath if he's rank. Most importantly, if you haven't both been tested for STIs and come out clean, use a flavoured condom. STI transmission via oral sex is on the increase.

Cheesy bloke hell: Sara's story

I met this man who was quite interested in me, to say the least. I didn't really fancy him but was flattered at the attention because he was incredibly rich and considered quite a catch. More to the point, I was drunk, so I wasn't really thinking straight.

We went up to my room and began kissing. Soon things began to get intimate and he pushed my head down so I could start sucking him. As I neared it, I had to fight back the urge to recoil in horror. He smelt – bad. More to the point, he was so posh his smegma smelt of blue cheese, which I've never liked at the best of times. I valiantly soldiered on but wish I hadn't because every time I remember the experience I feel ill.

Listen to his moans to see what he likes best. Lots of men like their frenulum – the 'stringy bit' under the head of their cock – to be teased or flicked with a tongue. Some men like having their balls played with, so you can put one hand to good use toying with his balls – gently – at the same time as sucking him and masturbating his shaft.

If you'd like to try 'deep-throating', learn how to control your gag reflex. You can make things easier by raising your 'soft palate'. Tense your mouth, flare your nostrils and you'll feel it rise. This gives more space for his penis to slide down. The more space your throat has got the better, so it's far easier to do it with your neck straight than bent, with him leaning over you while you pull him towards your face rather than vice versa.

Bear in mind that there are some men who are just too big to deep-throat. If this is the case, give him a similar sensation by lubricating your hand and then masturbating him with it while you push the head of his penis into your cheek. Most men can't tell the difference in the heat of the moment.

Asking him what he enjoys and then doing it (assuming you like what he suggests) is the best way of ensuring you both have fun. If you're really unsure of your technique, try acting out a fantasy where you are a sex novice and he has the job of instructing you. It can be a sexy way of improving your technique. And, of course, once you've learned what he likes, it's your turn to be teacher and show him what you like ...

Men's erogenous zones

You might think that men only have one erogenous zone – the cock – but if you want to be a truly sensational shag, get a bit more creative. Explore every inch of his body and not only will he think you're fantastic in the sack, but he'll be more inclined to return the favour, which has got to be a good thing.

- *Scalp*: There's loads of tension stored in the scalp, and a good head massage will make most men melt as you relieve all of their stress. Scalp massage can easily be incorporated into your love-action; start with a shoulder rub and move up.

  One of the easiest ways to give a scalp massage is sitting in an armchair while he leans back with his head between your thighs (never a bad idea). If you've got long nails, try gently scratching his scalp, or just rub the pads of your fingers over his head, letting them trail seductively down his neck. It can also be good the morning after, helping with hangover recovery. Try washing his hair in the shower and, as he recovers, you may get to take advantage of his morning horn.

- *Ears*: Assuming he's not some revolting mess who stores enough ear-wax to keep a candle factory supplied (if he is, what the hell are you doing shagging him?) the ears can be used to your advantage. Nibble lightly, suck and blow in and around his ears (don't shove your tongue in there unless you're sure he loves it). Whispering lewd suggestions can deliver a double-whammy; your warm breath and hot fantasies combining for a tantalising tease.

- *Lips*: One of the advantages of casual sex is that you get to snog loads of blokes, so make sure your pucker delivers some punch. Don't just plant your lips on his. Tease him by running your tongue sensually over his lower lip, alternate the pressure of your kissing and grip his bum as you snog him, grinding your pelvis against him at the same time. Try gently biting his lower lip, or suck it into your mouth. Dot tiny kisses over his mouth. Experiment with different snogging styles to become the kissing queen.

- *Neck*: The neck is a much under-rated erogenous zone, but soft kisses trailed all over it will make most men weak at the knees. Don't even think of giving him a love-bite — what are you, fifteen? It's marking your territory, which is just not cool.

- *Shoulders*: Mmmm, shoulders; few things are nicer than gripping onto a man's broad shoulders as you're getting it on. As well as using shoulder rubs to get a guy into the sack, get creative with them during sex. When you're on top and shagging him, let your hair brush against his shoulders (only if it's long, obviously. He'll think you're impersonating a cat if you try it with short hair). Dig your fingers – but not fingernails unless you're sure he likes it – into his shoulders as he shags you to show how much you're loving it.

- *Elbows*: Bet you didn't know that caressing the inside of the elbows can get a man horny. Lick or softly stroke the crook of the elbows, or follow the vein on his arm up to his elbows, glancing up every so often to show him that you're thinking of kissing something else with a big vein shortly.

- *Fingers*: Good old finger sucking; it's a cliché but men love it because it makes them think of oral sex (then again, what doesn't?). If you can keep a straight face, look him in the eye as you do it, to show him in no uncertain terms that you're a woman who really enjoys sucking on things.

- *Chest*: Some men have sensitive nipples and others don't but, unless you give them a tweak, you'll have no idea which category your bloke falls into. Try licking them as you kiss down his body en-route to delivering the perfect blow job, or gently pinch them with one hand while the other strokes his cock. Vary the pressure to see what he likes. And don't ignore the rest of his chest. Sit astride him and rub his chest all over before asking him to turn over so you can massage his back.

- *Back:* Some men hate being massaged but many find it erotic. Knead, stroke and slide your hands over his back. Using lube or talcum powder will make things easier. Avoid oil as it can get transferred from your hands to a condom and make them break. The coccyx, or dimple above his buttocks, is also very sensitive. Never press directly onto the spine though, as this can be dangerous.

- *Buttocks*: We spend loads of time eyeing them up and lots of men love having them groped. Massage his bum or grip it when you're snogging him to pull him towards you. Some men like it if you run your nails over their arse when you're shagging.

- *Penis*: Shock, horror — men like having their knob touched. And you thought you knew everything there was to know about sex. The glans/head is generally the most sensitive part of the penis. Run your thumb over it when you're wanking him, or lick it while your hand strokes his shaft.

  Pay particular attention to the corona (the ridge that runs all the way around the head of the penis) and the frenum (sometimes called the frenulum), which is the 'stringy' bit underneath the head, as many men find these particularly sensitive.

  Stroking the shaft with a steady rhythm will usually do the trick; try adding some lube to make things even better. However, wipe most of it off before you have sex as lube can make a condom more likely to slip off.

- *Scrotum and testicles*: The scrotum is the 'sack' that holds his balls. Some men find that it's too sensitive to touch but others really love it. Handle his scrotum and testicles with care though, as they're delicate things and easy to hurt.

  Try licking them or — very gently — taking one or both of them into your mouth to suck on, while your hand strokes his shaft. Trail your tongue over his scrotum or fondle his balls with your hands.

- *Perineum*: This is the area between his penis and anus, and ideal to add extra thrills without having to shove your finger up his arse and go for the prostate.

  Try pressing against the perineum with the heel of your hand while you're blowing or wanking him. Or use the fingers of one hand to massage it while the other strokes his shaft.
- *Anus and prostate*: You may rule this out altogether (and if you're not sure about his personal hygiene then it's definitely best avoided). It's also one erogenous zone that you really should ask first about; some men are super-squeamish about their anus being stimulated. You probably wouldn't like it if he dived into your arse without asking first, so you're just being polite.

  If you do dare to enter where the sun doesn't shine, you can stimulate his prostate, often described as the 'male G-spot'. This is a small gland about the size of a walnut, a few inches inside on the front wall. It responds to pressure applied through the rectum. Go gently, use lots of lube and make sure your nails are short so that you don't tear the delicate skin. Wearing a latex glove is also best for ultimate safety.

Alternatively, use a small toy or butt plug to stimulate his prostate (remember to wash it, or get him to, after use).

- *Thighs*: Men's thighs can be just as sensitive as women's. Work your way up from his feet to his thighs, gently blowing on his balls as you nibble his thighs. Be careful, though. He might be ticklish.

- *Knees*: Another one from the left-field, but men's knees are full of nerve endings so kiss and stroke the backs of his knees to give him a thrill.

- *Toes and feet*: Yeah, OK, men's feet aren't exactly the sexiest things in the world, tough toenails and cheesy smells never being top of any sensualist's list. But if you're feeling generous, give the guy a foot rub. Reflexologists claim that parts of the foot are linked to parts of the body, so give it a go and see which bits really get him going.

Some say that bending a man's toes back at the point of orgasm can enhance his pleasure.

Don't go for the toe-sucking thing unless you're really sure he's clean; you don't want to end up with toe-cheese in your mouth.

Advanced tricks and techniques

You've perfected your pump-action and can blow him away with your oral skills. Now's the time to start showing off. If you want a guy to leave your bed believing you're the best lover in the world, try incorporating something a bit special into your love action; a sex toy show, dressing up, striptease, anal sex or even fisting.

Don't ever do something that you feel uncomfortable with, and never go for any activity that requires trust unless it's someone you genuinely can trust; anal sex and fisting aren't things to try with strangers.

And don't feel obliged to do any of these things. Men are grateful enough if they get laid, and incredibly satisfied if they get a blow-job too, so you won't be disappointing them if you don't pull out any porn star tricks. Indeed, some men will be petrified if you get too wild, so judge your conquest carefully before you move on to anything too advanced.

Dressing up

If you're already in the heat of the moment then slipping out to change outfits probably isn't worth the effort. If, however, you've just put in a call to your fuck-buddy, opening the door wearing a sexy outfit can add an extra frisson (put a robe on top just in case it's not him).

I once spent an enlightening night as a kissogram girl. At the interview, I was told that the two most popular outfits that men went for were Miss Whiplash and Naughty Nurse; and the response these outfits got seemed to bear this out. Luckily, both are easy enough to create.

Talking dirty

As a general rule, talking dirty falls into five main categories. First, there's praising a body part; 'You're so big/hard/big and hard.' (Never underestimate the power of keeping things simple.) Then there's praising technique; 'I love the way your hands feel on my tits'.

Next comes descriptive stuff; 'Soon, I'm going to suck you until you come for me'. Then there's direction-giving; 'Play with my nipples while I wank you'. And finally there's fantasy-based stuff; 'You're my bitch, now'. Be careful not to go too far into your own fantasies unless you're sure that he shares them. Otherwise it could have the opposite effect to the one you're after.

Similarly, don't get too cheesy; 'Pump me till I squeal,' will make any self-respecting man collapse in hysterics, which is never good for spurring on orgasm.

For a Miss Whiplash look, almost any little black dress, or black top and skirt combo, will do. Add fishnet stockings and long gloves. If you want to get really into character, your local hardware store will come in handy; they sell chain of all types by the metre, so buy a piece long enough to tie your man up, fasten it round your waist with small padlocks and then hang a pair of hand-cuffs from your makeshift chain belt. All you need then is a whip. You can get these for a fraction of the price that sex shops sell them for if you go to a horse-riding supply shop. Or just buy one of the small and 'gentle' whips designed for sub/dom newbies. You're going for a look rather than actually getting into spanking action (though if you want to get into spanking, that's covered later) so it doesn't need to be expensive.

To live out his naughty nurse fantasies, you can either buy an outfit from most sex shops, or create your own by buying a nurse's bag from your local toy shop and teaming it with a plain white shirt-waister dress. Adding a sponge so that you can give him a bed bath is a nice touch too.

Other good and easy kinky outfits are bunny-girl (leotard plus bunny ears and a fluffy tail), schoolgirl (assuming that you can deal with the Lolita image it conjures up: if he asks you to shave your pubes as well then you may be dealing with a bloke who's got way too dodgy fantasies), or French maid (add an apron and little white handkerchief hat to a black skirt/white top combo). Or keep it simple: most men get turned on when they see a woman in stockings and suspenders. And if you learn how to take them off sexily, you'll arouse your man even more.

Striptease

OK, most men are happy if you get naked, but if you can do it with class then you'll impress him even more, not to mention help him live out his lap-dancer fantasies. Start by picking out some music that makes you feel horny; perhaps rock for a wild routine, soul or blues for sensual moves or any song with relevant words. Use as many tracks as you like, take your time and make sure that you build up the excitement. The tease is just as important as the strip.

Make sure that you've got enough space to strip; you won't look very sexy if you trip over the coffee table or go crashing into a plant. And turn those radiators up; there's nothing sexy about goose-pimples — and if your man gets too hot, you can always help him out of his clothes.

Set the mood with low lighting, but don't even think of using candles. They may give an erotic ambience but if you're flinging your clothes off with abandon, it can be dangerous; you want to be lighting your man's fire, not setting your house on fire. A table lamp, fairy lights or a lava lamp are far safer options.

Pick your clothes carefully. If something's difficult to remove then don't even think of trying to strip out of it. Avoid zips that you can't reach easily, awkward buttons and Velcro. It's effective for stripping but can snag stockings.

Similarly, your shoes should be comfortable so that you can dance in them (but sexy heels rather than Birkenstocks). Slip-ons such as court shoes are best if you intend to take off your stockings. Be careful with mules as they can slip off.

Decide whether you're going to go for a persona or just want to wear a slinky frock with stockings. If you do go with a persona, pay attention to detail. Make your hair and make-up match your image; heavy eyeliner and an 'up' do for a dominatrix, say, or bunches and painted-on freckles if you're a schoolgirl. Don't forget the accessories. Depending on your persona, you may want to add long evening gloves, a feather boa, a hat or even a wig.

Practise your routine in front of the mirror before you try it on anyone else. What feels sexy may not look sexy, so watch yourself closely. Look at any item of clothing that you're removing, as it draws the man's eyes to the relevant body part.

Go slowly. If you rush it then you're ignoring the whole point of striptease. You don't want to give everything away at once; you want him to be desperate for you to remove each item before you actually take it off.

Stroke any areas of naked flesh as you uncover them, and revel in the sensation. Make it clear with your expression that he'll get to touch you later – if he shows enough enthusiasm in your performance. Don't forget facial expression. Looking your man in the eyes while you're stripping will make his temperature soar, particularly if you think horny thoughts while you gaze at him. Smile too; it shows that you're enjoying yourself. Believe that you're sexy and you'll look sexy, which is what it's all about.

If you really want to up your pulling power, a striptease course is well worth the investment as you'll learn how to move your body in an utterly seductive way and remove your clothes with style. But even better, many of the moves can be subtly incorporated into the way you move on a day-to day basis; bending seductively to take a shot at pool, say, or peeling off your evening gloves at a posh event in such a way as to get men fighting over who's going to buy you the champagne!

If you find that striptease appeals to your exhibitionistic side, you may want to take things further, once you're naked …

Toys for two

Practically every man gets off on seeing women masturbate; maybe it's from seeing it in so many porn movies or perhaps it's because they like seeing something 'secret' and 'taboo'. Whatever the reason, it's worth noting that using a toy in front of a man can be very different from using it alone. While he will no doubt love seeing you with a vibrator, no matter what you're doing with it (within reason), a few tricks can make sure that he's remembering you for months after you've had your wicked way with him. And getting good word of mouth is a great way to get laid.

- *Spread 'em*: Yep, it's as lewd as it sounds. Men are visual and the more they can see, the more excited they get. So, when you're using your toy, spread your legs and, if you're particularly dextrous, use the fingers of one hand to part your labia while the other hand slides the toy in and around your bits.
- *Double the fun*? If you're anally inclined, then give him a show he'll never forget. Slide a toy into your vag, and then slip a smaller — well-lubed — toy into your anus. This is best done 'doggy-style' to give him the ultimate view.
- *Share the joy*: Start off using the toy on yourself, then ask your man to take over. You're combining battery-operated appliances with sex; what man isn't going to get excited?

A word of warning; some men are too insecure about their bits to want to see you with a huge vibrator. If you're unsure as to where your man stands, use a tiny toy rather than a maxi-vibro-dong as it will be far less off-putting. Or just use your fingers; they're unlikely to be bigger than his cock (with any luck).

Anal action

There's more to anal action than just anal sex. The anus is rich in nerve endings and stimulating it in the right way can make a man feel fab. You may want to stroke it gently with a well-lubed finger (use the same techniques as are suggested in the anal masturbation section in Chapter 2) or you might want to go for 'rimming' (licking the anus).

Before you go 'Euuuuugh', set aside your prejudice. Firstly, any anal play should start with a thorough wash, so you won't be dealing with anything nasty lurking there. And secondly, you shouldn't rim someone without using a dental dam (square of latex to cover the area – make one by cutting the tip off a flavoured condom then cutting down the side, or buy them from a sex shop) as otherwise you'll be opening yourself up to all manner of infections. So all you're really doing is licking a bit of rubber; how grim can that be?

When you're rimming, vary the pressure, from light darts of the tongue around the anus to firmer poking of the tongue into the anus (through the dental dam, being careful not to break it). You may even want to combine rimming with some anal fingering, but make sure that the dam remains in between your tongue and the anus.

Then there's the old 'prostate stimulation' thing – loved by some men and loathed by others, so check first. Assuming your man's game (and your nails are trimmed), put on a pair of latex gloves, lube up and rub your finger around his anus to relax it, only slipping your finger inside at all when the anus starts to open for you. Take things slowly: forcing the issue will only hurt.

As you get further inside his anus, start feeling around for the prostate. As explained before, it's a few inches inside, on the front wall and feels like a lumpy walnut. Stroking this will make a man gibber incoherently, and probably shoot his load.

And then there's the biggie: anal sex. For some reason, a huge amount of men are obsessed by anal, probably because it's in almost every porn vid ever made. Don't do it if you don't like it. You won't be relaxed, and being uptight is the enemy of enjoyable anal action. Stress tightens the sphincter – the bit a man needs to get past when he's going for backdoor action.

If a man gets pushy, either kick him out – life's too short to waste on pushy losers – or say 'I will if you will,' and get out your biggest vibrator. It tends to put most men off pretty quickly. (If it doesn't, put a condom on the vibe before you use it on him.)

Always use condoms for anal sex, and use a vat of lube (possibly two). Make him spend time warming up your arse first, too. You wouldn't let a bloke fuck you without getting you nice and wet, so he shouldn't expect you to take it up the jacksy without some foreplay first. The anus doesn't self-lubricate, but it will relax, which will make things far more enjoyable for both of you.

Take it like a man: strap on sex

Many men balk at the idea, but with the whole metrosexuality thing taking hold, and people generally getting more broad-minded, there are some blokes out there who like the idea of being shagged by a woman. Obviously, you don't have the equipment — but with the help of a strap-on, you soon can.

A strap-on is a sex-toy combining a dildo or vibrator with a harness that's worn around the waist or hips. The harness has a triangular or rectangular front piece that sits over a woman's vulva, and the front piece has a special opening to slip a flare-based dildo into. This gives you an artificial penis, so that you can penetrate, rather than be penetrated.

About 30 per cent of strap-ons sold by sex shops go to straight couples, so you don't need to feel like some kind of freak. However, strap-ons can take time for you both to get used to. The dildo needs to be fitted into the front piece and straps may need to be adjusted. Be patient, and bear in mind that you may feel awkward at first.

As with all anal play, make sure that you use lots of lubricant, on both the toy and the anus, and spend some time on anal foreplay before you get into full-on penetration. Treat him as you'd like to be treated. At first, hold back from thrusting, letting the bloke slowly accept the strap-on, instead of being actively penetrated. Don't feel like you have to make him take it all at once, either. He may only be able to take the tip of the toy the first few times.

Be aware that a man may get 'culture-shocked' from taking a more 'passive' role in sex, so he might feel vulnerable or even cry. If he does, he's not a wuss – he just needs a hug.

NB: Some people like trying simulated fellatio, in which the bloke sucks on the dildo. If it's previously been inserted anally, it should be thoroughly washed with soap and water before it enters the recipient's mouth.

Some women find anal sex easiest before they achieve orgasm, while they're still at the peak of arousal so, if your guy keeps you constantly 'on the edge', you may find it more enjoyable.

Once you're suitably warmed up, get into position. While doggy-style may be the one that automatically springs to mind, it's not necessarily the best, as it tends to make your muscles tighten up. As a more comfortable alternative, try anal sex with the man standing behind you, with his legs outside yours. This keeps your legs closer together, which, rather than making things tighter like it does with vaginal sex, actually loosens the anus as there's less pressure on it. You'll still need to take things slowly though, as the approach changes the angle at which the penis penetrates the anus, and it can be easy for him to start banging away with no concern for your poor backside.

It may sound complicated but the missionary position is the best position for anal as your muscles are more relaxed. For ease of penetration, vary it slightly; lie on your back with your knees in the air. Get your bloke to kneel or lie facing you and then slide in. You can use pillows to help raise your hips up to the optimum angle. With practice, you should find it entirely possible to have anal sex in 'normal' missionary style. And side-by-side is another good position for anal action. It's easier to relax your muscles and the man can play with your clit and breasts as he shags you.

Woman on top may seem ideal for anal as it puts you in more control, and you can decide the pace and depth you're happy with. However, it tightens your anus, making penetration trickier. If you try anal sex this way, lower yourself very slowly. The man should resist the urge to push up, as this can be painful; tell him beforehand and emphasise the point by keeping your hands on his hips while you're at it.

Don't do anal with a man you don't know that well; save it for fuck-buddies or regular shags. You need to be able to stop the bloke at any point and, if it's a one-night stand, you can't guarantee he'll listen because he'll be too caught up in the heat of the moment. Or he's a thoughtless idiot.

If the whole idea of anal sex turns you off, don't do it. Only ten per cent of couples do it – and that's people who are in a relationship. You shouldn't feel obliged to give your anus to someone on a brief encounter, unless it's something that you enjoy too.

Fisting

See section on self-fisting in Chapter 2. Just add your man in latex gloves and, as with anal, only let him do it if you really trust him.

Getting what you want in bed

Pleasuring a man perfectly is all very well, but you want to make sure that you enjoy the brief encounter as much as he does – if not more. Let him know if he touches you in a way you particularly enjoy, and warn him if you've got any inverse-erogenous zones that you loathe having touched, ideally before he touches them. That way, he'll know that it's about you, not him, and won't feel insecure (insecurity being the enemy of the erection). Expecting a man to read your mind is naïve; as Elvis didn't quite say, try a little less action, and a little more conversation. If you're comfortable enough with a guy to let him get squelchy with you then you shouldn't feel ashamed of telling him where to squelch.

You should also be ballsy enough to take any embarrassing situations in your stride; fanny-farts, cramp and strange odours can all form part of the sex experience, so get used to being blasé about it. You'll seem far cooler that way. No matter what happens, you can guarantee that something at least that bad has happened to someone else before.

A dirty job?

Worried about poo being involved when it comes to anal? There's no need to panic. As long as the recipient has emptied their bowels relatively recently, there shouldn't be any in the bit that you're poking away at (or having poked). Excrement stays in the colon, which is far higher up than the rectum.

To avoid any risk of gross-out factor, it is worth putting dark towels down on the bed before you start any form of anal play. That way, if you do encounter anything lurking, you can wipe it away without messing up your sheets. And if you wear latex gloves or if he wears a condom, not only is it safer but you can also deal with any fall-out by just peeling off the latex when you've finished and putting it in the bin.

It popped out: Jenner's story

Andy and I were old flames with a serious history of rampant sessions so, when he called to say he was in town for the night, I was more than happy to meet up with him. After a few drinks, it was apparent that the juices still flowed rather too freely, so we wandered back to his place for a 'coffee'.

Always the gentleman, Andy insisted on several hours of foreplay then produced a vibrator. Giggling and squealing ensued. After hours of fun, we eventually got down to full-on fucking, working our way through a couple of packs of condoms, which he slobbishly disposed of on the floor.

Morning came too quickly (unlike him), and soon it was time for him to catch his train back. We decided to have one last shag before he left. On went the condom. He leaned over me and was just about to put it in when he yelled 'Call me an ambulance!' Not what I expected. I figured he was joking – until I saw the pain on his face and rapidly shrinking dick. Apparently, he'd got a history of dislocating his shoulder and putting weight on it could pop it out of its socket. There then came the dilemma of how to move from underneath him without further dislocating his shoulder. This wasn't helped by my difficulty in breathing (me, 5 foot 6 inches and slim; him, 6 foot 4 inches and stocky). After much struggling, I escaped to the phone.

'Hi, I'd like an ambulance please.'

'Why?'

'My friend's dislocated his shoulder.'

'How?'

The operator tried not to laugh. She failed.

After twenty minutes, the ambulance crew arrived. I'd just about managed to divest him of his condom and get him into his boxers. The crew came upstairs, took one look at him, near-naked and groaning, glanced around the condom-littered room and smirked. Then I noticed the vibrator in the middle of the floor. Trying nonchalantly to throw a sweatshirt over a vibrator without raising any suspicions doesn't work. Especially when it starts buzzing (no, I'm not joking).

By the time we got to the hospital, the ambulance crew had proudly announced its find to the entire ambulance staff, who were openly laughing as we walked past. Andy got asked by five separate consultants how the mishap occurred. I got redder and redder.

The final straw was when the female doctor walked into the cubicle. Taking one look at his sweaty and semi-clad form, she commented, 'It's a good thing this didn't happen five minutes later'. He was too off his head on anaesthetic to respond. I tried desperately to look unconnected to the whole incident.

On the plus side, for the next month he was laid up in bed totally helpless. And although he took a lot of convincing, we finally got to have that one last shag without dislocating anything else.

If he's not hitting the spot at all, don't be tempted to fake it. Compliments always go further than criticism, so say 'Mmmm, I love that' when he gets it right. Stay silent or wriggle away when he gets it wrong so that he gets an idea of your body's blueprint. If he's miles off the mark, reposition his hand or murmur that you love being touched softly on your [insert preference here]. You can incorporate it into talking dirty if you're confident with that kind of thing, to add extra thrills. Be honest and don't say what you think he wants to hear. Gasping 'harder, faster' like some porn chick is counter-productive if you really want him to grind slowly against you.

If he gets into the spirit of things and starts telling you what he wants, tell him if he uses a word you hate. You may be able to put up with him asking you to stroke his 'love-muscle' when you're indulging in foreplay, but it could scare away your orgasm if he uses the same word during sex. Orgasms are elusive enough things at the best of times so don't let him do anything to discourage them.

Do me, baby

You'll know when the time is right to move on to fucking; namely, after you've both had enough foreplay. Now's the time to put the condom on him. No matter what a man's size or sensitivity, there will be one out there to suit him. Not only will condoms help protect you against STIs but they can help the man to last longer. Indeed, Trojan and Durex both make condoms with a small amount of anaesthetic inside to help prolong his performance.

If you've done the whole 'practising on a banana' thing, you might want to put it on with your mouth. Make sure it's flavoured if you're trying it this way, as normal condoms taste foul.

Alternatively, try giving him a hand job and, just as he's getting close, slide the condom on, making sure to use the hand that hasn't been in contact with his bits. A drop of lube in the tip of the condom will make it more sensitive for him too. You could try putting the condom on while your man's distracted; say, when you're in the 69 position and he's too busy focusing on your bits to notice what's going on downstairs. Slipping it on then flipping round and sliding on to his cock will prevent any of the 'mood-spoiling' that some people worry about.

Remember, the condom should go on well before his cock goes anywhere near your bits. Not only will it help keep you safe from STIs, but remember, the average penis has three million sperm on the tip before you start getting jiggy, and it only takes one to get you pregnant.

Sex positions

You might just want to stick with the same old, same old when you're having sex, but if you're tarting around then why not add extra variety with some different positions?

Not only will it keep things interesting if you're getting laid every night of the week, but different positions can be used to make the most – or least – of a man's assets.

Don't feel bad about insisting on whatever your favourite sex position may be. He's a guy so, chances are, he's going to come (unless he's one of those blokes who can't come through penetrative sex, in which case the position is irrelevant to him anyway). You're a woman, so you'll probably need your buttons pressed just that bit more precisely. And any decent guy will be more than happy to oblige; after all, he's getting laid, which is probably enough for him.

Tiny todger sex positions

You've been fondling away, hoping that he's a 'grower' rather than a 'shower', but now you've got him up to full stretch – and he's still tiny. What to do? Well, if you're a real size queen, you could send him home and give the poor lad a complex for life. But if you've fancied him up to this point, don't give up. There are positions that will make sure he can still hit the sides, even if he makes a chipolata look large.

- *Boosted missionary*: Lie on your back, legs spread and knees bent, with the man on top of you. Once he's slid inside, put your feet on his thighs or buttocks. He won't have as much control over thrusting as in the traditional missionary position, but penetration is far deeper when you bend your legs. The higher up your body you put your feet, the deeper he'll get. As well as emphasising every inch he has, this position also pushes his pubic bone against your clitoris and helps give you maximum stimulation. You can push him deeper inside you by controlling his thrusts with your feet. Be careful if the man has a bad back, though, as the pressure on his buttocks may be too much for him.

- *Bum lift*: Again, lie back with your legs spread. The man then puts his hands under your hips and lifts them up to best angle his penis towards your G-spot. He should also spread his legs as this takes the pressure off his testicles, ensuring they're not too squashed to feel stimulated. Now, rest your legs on the man's arms or shoulders. Again, the higher you raise them, the deeper he gets and the bigger he'll feel.

  This position gives your man a great view, as he can see everything that's happening very clearly, which can increase arousal, making him harder. He can also stroke your breasts and clit to give you some extra stimulation.

- *On the edge*: Lie on your back, dangling your legs and thighs over the edge of a bed, sofa, kitchen table, office desk, or wherever else appeals. Spread your legs, putting one on the floor. Get the bloke to lie on top, with one leg on the floor and the other kneeling on the bed/whatever other surface. Now wrap the leg that isn't resting on the floor around his waist. This deepens penetration and helps give you some control over the thrusts. He can stroke your breasts and clit while you're fucking, or you can use a vibe on your clit while he thrusts away. Then again, if you have a small man and a big vibrator, you may just want to kick him out and sort yourself out instead.

Love-python sex positions

It's not just small cocks that can be problematic. Dealing with a man who's hung like a horse can be deeply uncomfortable (literally), leading to 'cervix in the throat' syndrome, where you're convinced he's going to break your bits at any moment. But the right position can work wonders to minimise a man's meat. That, and a hell of a lot of foreplay; when you're seriously turned on, the cervix tilts backwards slightly, getting it further out of the way of a thrusting cock.

• *Reverse CAT (Coital Alignment Technique)*: Start in the traditional woman on top position, with the man's cock inside you only as deep as is comfortable. Gradually move until you're lying directly on top of him. By gently rocking and circling your hips, your clitoris and pubic area get maximum stimulation while his penis stimulates you inside. Close your legs for maximum pleasure. Because you're controlling things, you can decide how deep he gets to go, and the angle means that he won't be able to get every last inch inside you, no matter how hard he pushes.

- *Flat doggie*: A big boy who wants it doggie style; what could be worse? But don't worry, with a bit of tweaking, this position is entirely possible. Rather than kneeling on all fours, just lie flat on the bed with the guy behind you. He can slide in easily but penetration is shallower than with traditional doggie, so you should find it easier to cope.

- *Standing sex*: If a bloke's huge, forget wrapping your legs around his waist during standing sex. Instead, stand on a telephone book or on a stair higher than him, so that you're at the right height for him to penetrate you. He can then slide in without slipping you his full length. This is a great position for when you've just got back from the pub and fancy a quickie.

NB: As with anything sexual, the golden rule is, if you don't like something, ask your partner to stop. It's supposed to be fun for both of you, after all.

Kinks and how to deal with them

If you're shagging the planet, chances are you're going to run into at least one person — and probably more — who has some kind of kink. Sub/dom, bondage, foot fetishism, spanking, water-sports; they're all out there and new ones seem to spring up all the time. Even if you've got no intention of getting kinky, it's worth knowing about what's out there so you know exactly what it is you're being asked to do (and how offended you should be).

Alternatively, you could have a kink that you want to indulge. Just because you're having casual sex, it doesn't mean that you have to keep things vanilla. But how can you introduce it without terrifying a guy or coming across as a weirdo? You can try pulling in 'scene' places or meeting people through fetish websites but, as well as limiting the embarrassment factor, it'll also limit your pulling chances. If handled with enough grace and class, you should be able to at least introduce the subject of your fetish without terrifying a man; and if you're lucky, he'll be game for some experimentation.

Group sex

What is it?

Oh, come on! Fairly obviously, it's sex with more than one other person. It's so common nowadays that it barely qualifies as a kink (probably something to do with the Ecstasy generation getting down to it and paving the way for everyone else to follow). Group sex is best tried when you're doing the casual thing; if you try it in a relationship, it has a huge potential for heartbreak unless you're both very sure that it's for you.

The most common form of group sex is troilism, aka the threesome: two men and a woman (MMF) or two women and a man (FFM). Many men spend their adult life praying for the latter.

What to do if he asks for it?
If he wants to go for it but you don't, you can still go some of the way to satisfying the fantasy. Watch a girl/girl porn movie with him, or record yourself having an orgasm and/or talking dirty, then play it during sex so that he can imagine there's another woman there.

You can also spray a different perfume to your normal one on one side of the bed; the different smell will help him imagine there are two women there if he closes his eyes. Or try blindfolding him, then sitting on his face and writhing, while you masturbate him (ideally with a different rhythm) to give his imagination more ammunition. Wearing a glove on one hand and keeping the other one bare will work in a similar way. And if he likes the idea of a boy/boy/girl combo, just add sex toys to the equation.

What to do if you want it
If you decide that you do want to bite the bullet and go for group sex, but your current shag-piece won't play, there are various places to find other people who will. Never try to get someone drunk to coerce him or her into group action (or any other kind of sex). Just look elsewhere.

There are numerous organisations that run swinging events and parties, and as a single woman you'll be in hot demand — particularly if you're bi (or bi-curious). Some events are sex-free and simply allow you to chat to like-minded people and make your own arrangements. Others are more full-on, with actual sex likely to happen at the events.

Swinging websites are also a good source of people to play with; many have bulletin boards where you can place requests, but make sure you read the 'frequently asked questions' section of the site first to make sure you don't contravene any of their guidelines.

Other hints and tips
Make sure that you play it safe, particularly if you're meeting people you don't know. Apply the same rules as you would for online dating; tell someone where you're going and have a friend ready to call you after a set amount of time to check that you're safe. If you feel uncomfortable, leave immediately. Be aware of drink spiking too.

Assuming that you're safe, you'll probably want to have a few glasses of wine before you start to make sure you're relaxed, but set the ground-rules first — and definitely before you get naked. It might be that you only want to fool around rather than have full penetrative sex, or you might want to have a 'no double penetration' rule. Decide beforehand and you shouldn't run into any problems.

Make sure that you use condoms and dental dams, and be careful about transferring fluids through a third party (for example, if you blow a bloke then go down on a woman you could be risking getting her pregnant or giving her an STI. Which isn't terribly sisterly behaviour, now, is it?)

Spanking

What is it?

Again, it's pretty self-explanatory. It's letting someone smack your buttocks — or you smacking theirs (public schoolboys are so much fun). Some people love it and others just giggle, but it's been part of sex for years. Even the *Kama Sutra* says 'Blows are a form of love-play.' And it's pretty common; 22 per cent of men say they like spanking a woman, and 20 per cent like being spanked lightly themselves (a further 13 per cent say they like to be spanked so that it hurts).

It's not just some weird power kick thing, although that can be a part of it. When you're spanked, your nerve endings send pain impulses called Substance P to the brain, which triggers endorphin release. The endorphins find the nerve endings that caused the release of Substance P and cap them, acting like a filter to stop the flow. This blocks pain so that the body can take on more or harder striking. As the slaps continue, this cycle repeats and, as more stimulation is applied, the amount of endorphins released can cause a euphoric state of mind.

What to do if he asks for it?

If he wants you to spank him, what's the harm? Let the poor boy have his kicks. Use the flat of your hand or get more advanced with a wooden spoon, paddle (looks like a table-tennis bat), slapper (like paddles but made from two pieces of leather that aren't sewn together at the end, so that they make a louder 'slapping' sound) or tawse (like slappers but cut to form 'fingers'). Build up intensity slowly, rather than going in hard to start with. As he gets used to it, you can up the pressure, but stop the second that he asks you to.

If a man asks to spank you, and you're happy with it, ask him to start gently and stop at any point you ask him to. Don't let any man spank you unless you trust him; you don't want to get hurt. Anyone who won't take no for an answer – graciously – isn't worth fucking.

What to do if you want it?

If you want to be spanked, start slowly; ask him to give your arse a slap during sex to get him used to the idea. Some men get freaked out about inflicting pain on a woman, so reassure him that it's something you definitely want. Once he's comfortable, you can up the ante and ask him for a full-on spanking session.

If you want to spank him, ask nicely. The worst he can do is say no. But no, you can't spank him for disobeying you if he does.

Other hints and tips

Spanking can be teamed with anal fingering, if you're spanking him, and vaginal and/or anal fingering if he's spanking you, to help trigger orgasm. If you want to get the kit to indulge his fantasy, the internet is your friend: you'll find anything you can possibly need.

She wanted me to hit her: Juan's story

We'd only been going out about three weeks when Suzie put it very bluntly: 'I'm totally submissive. I need you to spank me.' As a good middle-class liberal, I wasn't sure I even could; deliberately inflicting pain on the one you love? Fortunately, that fell to one side as she seductively pulled down her panties and laid herself across my legs.

The moment my hand connected with her arse, she made a noise that was more excited, fulfilled and outright horny than I'd heard in three weeks of penetrative sex. The more aroused she got, the harder I wanted to spank her, until I realised that, despite all my reservations, I was really enjoying myself. The feel of her grinding against my thigh, the warmth of her when I alternated spanking with driving two fingers roughly against her G-spot, and especially those noises, had my cock pressed hard into her abdomen, and that in turn was exciting her more. She came hard – while being spanked, not fingered – and I was sold on the idea.

Thank God for the internet. Several 'subs' [people into 'submissive' sex; see section on 'Power play' a few pages on] on a sex forum helped me come to terms with the fact that Suzie needed to be spanked. For them, it boiled down to the 'punishment' freeing them to enjoy sex. They also gave me a world of information about the perfect spanking. I knew about agreeing a 'safe word' that signals stopping immediately, but they suggested that, before we got down to it, I got permission to do things such as pull her hair, scratch her and use a hairbrush on her. This was about setting boundaries, but also reassuring her I was thinking it through and wouldn't go psycho and ignore the safe word. They also reiterated a key point I had already worked out: the spanking happens more in the spankee's head than her buttocks, so that was where to concentrate my efforts.

I felt a bit stupid growling out dominant language as Suzie squirmed on my lap in anticipation, but it was for her and it definitely did the trick. Sometimes I would wait until she begged to give her the first spank, sometimes I would surprise her. More advice from the subs: the first impact should always be exactly half as hard as the hardest you would dare. It gives you some room for manoeuvre as she gets more excited, but it shows you're serious. From then on it's a question of improvisation. I like to build up a rhythm so my spankee is expecting the next spank, then stop abruptly, only hitting her again when her body relaxes. Other things that work well are alternating buttocks, spanking her at the tops of her thighs (the most sensitive point is right where her buttocks become her legs), and using my fingers to penetrate roughly. I can't remember how many times it was impressed on me not to spank anywhere near the bottom of her spine.

The best trick I developed was to bring Suzie to the point of orgasm using my fingers, then pull out and spank her hard and fast. It brought her to a much bigger orgasm than just being fingered alone. After she collapsed I would put my fingers back in her and gently rub her G-spot. And the most important thing: after it was all over I collected her up in my arms and gave her a big hug. Not only was it a nice thing to do, but it closed the session and made it clear the 'dom' act was over.

Suzie and I split up for other reasons, but I still say a silent prayer of thanks to her every time I meet a submissive woman.

Bondage

What is it?

Another common kink, bondage is all about restricting movement. At the extreme end of things, people use cling-film, bondage beds or giant inflatable rubber suits. However, you're far more likely to meet people in the shallow end of the pervy pool, who just like the idea of being tied up with silk scarves or maybe handcuffed. And you're pretty damned likely to meet them; a recent Policy Exchange poll found that 38 per cent of Brits have experimented with bondage: more than in any other country.

The next most likely to try bondage are the Dutch, on 27 per cent. In Sweden the figure is 21 per cent and only 11 per cent of the French have dabbled.

What to do if he asks for it?
If he wants to tie you up but you're not sure, rather than going for ties or handcuffs, try a pair of feather handcuffs. These aren't strong enough to actually restrain you, but still give the feeling of being tied. Fake fur cuffs are a firmer, but still relatively gentle, option. However, don't do this unless you can trust him; any level of restraint is too much if you don't trust a bloke 100 per cent.

What to do if you want it?
No matter how into bondage you are, safety should always come first. Again, don't let a man tie you up unless you totally trust him; he can do anything once you're tied, and while that is partly the point, you don't want a virtual stranger having that kind of control over you. If you want to tie him up, start by pinning his hands above him when you're on top during sex. If he responds well, suggest moving on to tying him with silk scarves. From then, it's up to the pair of you how far you take things.

Other hints and tips
There's science behind the sexiness of bondage; pulling against restraints can build a rush of adrenaline and

euphoria. The brain is also thought to produce more alpha waves, creating a 'floating' state. This can induce come-downs, so don't be surprised if you're tearful after a bondage session.

If you're going to experiment with bondage, always have a safe word and make sure that you're with a partner who will untie you the second you use it. And you should never be left alone once you're tied, or leave anyone alone. A tied person should be constantly monitored for circulation, breathing, skin tone and temperature of the fingers and toes. And never tie anything around the neck or use slip-knots as these can tighten up and block off blood supply.

He went too far: Jemima's story

When I was a kid I was intrigued by those old black and white films where the dastardly villain with a handlebar moustache ties the innocent heroine on to a train track. I didn't see it as a sexual thing but, as I got older, I found my fantasies tended to involve some kind of tying up, usually by a villainous man.

I kept it to myself for a long time, enjoying the fantasy but feeling too embarrassed to ask a partner to do it. Then I had a long-term relationship with Gregory and we ended up exploring our fantasies together. I enjoyed the reality of being tied up as much as I'd enjoyed the fantasy; there's just something about being utterly in someone else's power.

When I became single, I went back to relying on my fantasies but, after a while, I met Jim. We fooled around with each other a few times but hadn't actually had sex; I need to have an emotional connection with someone to let them take that final step.

One night, we were talking about fantasies and I said I'd do anything that he wanted, except have sex. He said he wanted to tie me up, and my heart soared. I was naked in seconds. He turned me over and tied me doggy-style to the bed – then started to have sex with me. I asked him to stop, but he wouldn't.

By the time he finished, I was crying; I thought that I could trust him but he took advantage the second that he could. I kicked him out of the house and considered reporting him, but thought that the police would say that it was my own fault for letting him tie me up.

Now, I wouldn't let someone tie me up unless I knew them incredibly well. I'd thought that I could trust Jim after a few dates but that clearly wasn't enough for me to tell what he was really like.

Power-play

What is it?

Power-play can be divided into two main areas; submission and domination (sub/dom) and sadomasochism (S&M). While they're often lumped together, they are actually different things. Sub/dom is mostly in the mind; it's about controlling someone, usually with a threat of emotional or physical pain. Humiliation falls into sub/dom; for example, being made to wear a short skirt without undies, or making a guy tell you that he's your bitch.

Sadism, on the other hand, is about inflicting pain; think whips'n'chains'n'pointy things, candle wax, breast torture (sticking pins in tits. Mmm, nice). And masochism is enjoying pain; so, enjoying being whipped, chained or pointy-thinged.

Some people are pure sub, others are pure domme (or dom, if they're male) and yet others are switch; equally happy to give and receive.

What to do if he asks for it?
First of all, don't be surprised. According to male sexual fantasy book *My Secret Garden Shed*, you're more likely to run into a man who's into domination — 28 per cent of men are into it — but male subs aren't exactly rare, at 13 per cent. Queendom.com found that 42 per cent of men are interested in having hot wax dripped onto them, while Kinsey found that 50 per cent of people like being bitten during sex so it seems that pleasure and pain really do go together for a lot of people.

The good news is that you can enjoy power-play without getting into a scary world of men in gimp masks and women in thigh boots (then again, thigh boots can hide a multitude of sins). Try nipple pinching, hair pulling or back scratching, or get some massage candles from blissbox.com.

These soy wax candles melt at a safe and comfortable temperature so you get the thrill of candle-play without the burn. Judicious use of a blindfold will put your partner in control of you, or vice versa.

For more inspiration, get reading. *The Story of O* is a classic power-play text. Masochists will enjoy Masoch's *Venus in Furs*, and sadists can get some dark ideas from the original master, the Marquis De Sade.

What to do if you want it?

Tread carefully. Yet again, this is something that you should only incorporate in casual sex if you're utterly sure that you can trust whoever your with, and is thus best left for fuck-buddy or pseudo-relationship scenarios.

But that doesn't mean that you have to leave it alone entirely. Asking a bloke 'Am I your slut?' (if you can do it without giggling) will give him the idea that you like being treated mean. Conversely, if you notice his breath shorten when you whisper 'You're mine to do what I want with,' then you'll probably be safe to progress with a domme scenario. Just take it slowly; successful power-play is all about trust and intimacy. By its nature, casual sex may not be high on these things, so don't rush into anything that could end up going pear-shaped.

If your man isn't into it and you decide you want to experiment alone, it's safest going to an organised club night with like-minded people, as they have strict rules (well, they would, wouldn't they) so you're less likely to run into trouble. Club Wicked (clubwicked.org) runs regular BDSM (bondage, domination and sadomasochism) events in London, or check online for details of events in your area.

Other hints and tips
Handle all forms of power-play, even if purely verbal, with extreme care. Your brain releases hormones called endorphins when pain is inflicted. This is the body's natural form of morphine and is normally released in small amounts when you hurt yourself, to help alleviate the pain. During submission it's released in much larger doses, creating a natural 'high'. The endorphins released can inhibit pain-blockers, so take it slowly.

And while endorphin release can be fantastic, it comes with a down-side. As levels return to normal, you'll often experience a 'come-down', feeling confused or tearful. Your partner should help you cope with it by gradually bringing you back down to earth with smaller and smaller amounts of pleasure, so that you can slide back to 'normality' rather than crashing from a great height. Warn him you'll want extra cuddles when you've finished. If he's a swine who doesn't do as you asked, pamper yourself to help make the comedown easier; have a relaxing bath and masturbate to release more endorphins and help restore your hormone balance. No good sexual experience should leave you feeling sad.

Never indulge in any form of power-play unless you have a 'safe word'; something that you wouldn't normally say during sex, such as 'aubergine' (as saying 'no' or 'stop' can be part of the fun). When that word is said, everything stops without any questions or objections. If you're using candles, your partner should always keep the flame at least 30cm from your skin, and use unscented candles (not beeswax), as unscented wax melts at a lower temperature.

He was my bitch: Tina's story

I'd never encountered sub/dom other than on TV documentaries, so when Eric, a guy I'd had sex with a few times, asked me to dominate him, I was unsure as to what to do. I liked the idea of pleasing him but was nervous that he'd want me to hurt him. He explained that he liked being under a woman's power, but not physically damaged, so I decided to give it a go.

I got dressed up in a slinky black dress and high heels, then walked into the 'dungeon' (OK, my bedroom) where he was waiting. He was visibly aroused as he gasped, 'I'll do anything, Mistress. What do you want?'

I found it hard to keep a straight face and said the first thing that came into my head: 'Go to the corner shop and get me some fags and wine'. He looked a bit disappointed but did as he was told. I thought I could get used to this, but decided it would be too cruel to make him tidy my flat (though I found out later that some sub men get off on tidying up for women!).

When he returned, I tried to enter into my 'Mistress' persona, lighting a cigarette and pouring myself – but not him – a glass of wine. I ordered him to strip, which he did with inordinate haste, then tied him to the bed. I sat next to him, blowing smoke in his face and ordered him to tell me what he wanted. Every time he called me Mistress, I had to fight back the urge to giggle and, at one point, I had to go to the room next door because I knew I was going to crack up.

I ended up masturbating over his face with a sex toy but refusing to let him touch me. He then asked if he could lick it clean while I used another toy on him. I was a bit grossed out at the idea but got a vibrator, put a condom on it and started to slide it in and out of his anus as he licked the other toy that I'd masturbated with. He asked me to take a photo of him, which I did, but when he offered me a copy of the picture, I declined. The mental image will stay with me forever, and I really don't want a picture to remind me of what I did.

I'm glad that we gave it a go, because it helped him live out a fantasy that he'd always had, but it's safe to say that I'm not a natural dominatrix.

Foot fetishism

What is it?

There are several types of foot fetishism; your basic foot fetish; retifism, which is a love of shoes; and altocalciphilia, a love of high heels. The latter is thought to have started in the mid nineteenth century, when a prostitute took a pair of 'French heels' with her to a New Orleans brothel. The madam noticed that the men were willing to pay more for this prostitute, so ordered heels for all her girls. The trend spread through other brothels, and men started ordering them for their wives. So if it hadn't been for a hooker, there'd be no Manolos!

Heels make you seem more vulnerable, bringing out a man's protective urges or, more scarily, his 'predator' instinct, because you seem weaker. You walk in a more 'feminine' way, exacerbating the male/female power difference. Heels also change your posture, curving your spine, exaggerating the sway of your hips, and making your buttocks and calves seem curvier and your breasts push out more. Marilyn Monroe famously chopped a chunk off one of her heels to add to her famous wiggle.

High heels aside, according to queendom.com, 12 per cent of men like toe sucking, and four per cent like having their toes sucked. And according to Dr Pam Spurr, foot fetishism is one of the top three most common fetishes. 'The foot fetishist, in childhood, may have been pulled out of the bath, placed tummy down on his mum's lap and rubbed dry with the towel while staring at the floor – and her feet! As he was rubbed dry, he'd innocently receive stimulation to his genitals (pushed into his mum's lap as she towelled him dry) and so his fetish for feet was born. While staring at her feet he was aroused and the two were forever linked.'

There's science behind the attraction as well as psychology; it's a pheromone thing again. Every square centimetre of the sole of the foot has about 600 sweat glands – more than any other part of the body except the palm of the hand – so your feet are pheromone-rich.

What to do if he asks for it?

Don't be judgmental; he's probably found it hard to admit to. If the idea totally grosses you out, tell him – gently – but maybe let him paint your toenails as a special treat. After all, you'd pay for a pedicure, wouldn't you? You can also wear sandals when you go out, or make sure that he can see your feet during sex, so that he gets the additional stimulation without going anywhere near your tootsies.

If you decide you're going to give it a go but have ticklish feet, get him to give you a foot rub with firm pressure first, to prevent you from collapsing into giggles. Warn him, too, as you don't want to end up kicking him in the face (unless he's into that kind of thing!). Some women love having their toes sucked and others find it makes them unbearably squeamish; you won't know until you try. Ask him to take it slowly, so you can see whether or not it's for you.

If he's after a foot job, use lots of lube to make it easier, and try different positions. You may find it easiest to sit facing him on the bed, and slide both feet up and down his penis. Or you may find it easier to stand above him and rub your sole up and down his shaft. He'll have his own preferences, so ask him what he wants, and do whatever you can – comfortably – to oblige.

Some foot fetishists prefer it if you don't wash your feet before they worship them (though you may not want to kiss him after he's finished sucking your toe-cheese). It could be that he wants you to play with his feet, though foot fetishism is far more likely to work the other way round. If he does, consider giving him a foot massage; if he washes his feet first then that's no biggie. If he wants you to suck his toes and you're game, you may want to sweeten the deal with chocolate sauce or honey.

What to do if you want it?
There are many more male foot fetishists than female foot fetishists – possibly because women's feet are so much better looked after – but if you're one, start with 'low-end' activities such as a foot massage and work your way up from there. Respect his boundaries; there's no point engaging in sexual activities that your partner doesn't enjoy, and there are plenty of websites out there for you to get your kicks from.

Other hints and tips
If he's into heels, your man may want to be trampled or even have the heel of a stiletto inserted in his anus during

sex. Make sure you're well aware of the risks before you enter into this kind of play; you don't want the poor sod ending up in hospital.

Bear in mind that even professional dommes only tend to put one heel on their 'partner's' back, using the other to take their weight; you don't want to puncture his skin or damage his internal organs. If you're inserting anything into the anus, make sure that it's well lubricated and doesn't have any rough edges. It goes without saying that the heel should be clean. If the shoes have been worn outdoors, they could have all manner of bacteria on them.

Feet first: Woi's story

Sooner or later, any woman I sleep with will hear a particular phrase. 'This might sound silly, but … can I kiss your feet?' I don't know why, and from a Freudian perspective I'd rather not find out, but feet turn me on like nothing else. Worshipping a woman's feet is one of the most tactile, intimate and intense things you can do, second only to cunnilingus. It starts with the shape of the ball of her feet and her toes, through the pheromone-laced scent of shoe leather, to the contrast between the rough and smooth skin as I lick. Having a woman rub her feet in my face, force her toes into my mouth and stroke me with her soles is an erotic experience that shoots right for my hindbrain, bypassing reason and introspection.

The majority of women I've met have been quite happy to indulge me; I put this down to the fact that I bring my fetish up in a way that acknowledges it's really quite silly, and I make sure I ask the question after spending a lot of time tending to her needs. (I'm actually being a little bit selfish as I find having a wet chin after cunnilingus adds to the experience.) Only one woman has ever refused, I think out of fear for her ticklish feet. Some foot fetishists do get off on tickling their partner but I have spent time developing techniques that don't tickle, because the last thing I want is for my partner to jerk her foot while it's in my face!

One or two women I've known have really got into it – the ones who enjoyed having their toes sucked, coincidentally enough. The most amazing experience I've ever had was with a girlfriend who wore tights and boots to work all day, then sat on my thighs with my cock between her legs and her feet, still in the tights, in my face. Then she slowly jerked me off, and let me come on her legs. The memory of my cum soaking into the nylon will be with me for a very long time, I think.

On the other hand, there's nothing worse than a woman who does nothing with her feet while I'm worshipping them. For any fetishist the key attraction is the woman behind the feature he fetishises, and inert feet might as well be on a waxwork. I want a woman to grip my nose with her toes, flex her sole and wiggle her feet, tease me by running her feet up my body and stopping just short of my mouth … anything but lie there pretending it's not happening.

Advocates of foot fetish will tell you it's the most common fetish there is, which means there's a huge amount of variety in what people mean when they say they have one. Some men like to have a woman use a stiletto heel to torture their genitals and put weight on their testicles. I don't. So if you meet a foot fetishist, talk it over with them. They'll know what they want and if they have a lick of sense they'll be happy to share it. If they don't like to talk about it, start off gently and let them guide you. And get ready to be treated to foot rubs as often as you like …

Watersports

What is it?

Watersports, or 'urophilia', refers to people who take pleasure from acts involving urine. Generally, this is urinating on a partner, or being urinated on, although it can also involve drinking urine, either direct from source or from a glass. Eleven per cent of men have tried watersports, and a further 25 per cent like the idea, compared to 8 per cent of women who've tried it and a further 12 per cent who like the idea.

Men secrete androsterone, a sex hormone, in their urine, which may explain why some women enjoy it; some young women in Germany even used to add a few drops of urine to their husband's coffee as a 'love-spell'.

For men, watersports fetishism often originates in childhood; even if a guy's mum wouldn't let him touch his penis at any other time, chances are she let him hold it while urinating.

He may have also got a sense of power from 'who can pee the highest' games or learned that people retreat when threatened with being urinated on. This combination of power, rebellion and sensuality can be a heady mix.

If it's watching you urinate that gets him off, again, there's a natural explanation. Women tend to be presented as 'ladylike' and seeing you pee removes some of the 'mystery', making you seem more accessible.

What to do if he asks for it?
Fight back the urge to go 'Eurgh!' and consider how far you'd be prepared to go. Even if the idea of peeing on a man – or being peed on – fills you with dread, you could give him a kinky thrill if you just don't 'wipe' after urinating so that he can feel your urine in your pubic hair. Conversely, a bloke can wipe his urine onto you from his penis, if he doesn't 'shake' after urinating.

If you decide that you are willing to experiment, you may find it easiest to start in the bathroom; let your man put his hand under your stream of urine as you sit on the toilet, or hold his penis while he pees. It should go without saying that more advanced watersports can be messy, so put down newspapers or plastic sheets if you're trying it in the bedroom, or try it in the bath. Either partner can lie down in the bath (if it's filled with water then the warmth may make it easier for you to urinate). The other partner then, well, goes with the flow.

Even though the idea of watersports may appeal, bear in mind that you're going against heavy training *not* to urinate in front of someone else, so your body may not play ball. Make things easier on yourself by drinking lots of water; this will also help dilute your urine so it won't taste or smell as strong.

What to do if you want it?
Test the water (sorry) first by mentioning that it's something you've read about and are intrigued by. He may be horrified, so having a bit of distance from it will mean that you can gauge whether he's likely to play ball or not. If he is, follow the tips as above. If he's not, experiment with your own urine during masturbation, and check out the internet for sites about your kink.

Other hints and tips
Watersports can be useful for toning up your sex muscles; having good control over your pelvic muscles will help you control the stream of urine, stopping and starting easier. Get these muscles into shape by doing your Kegel exercises: flex and release your pelvic floor muscles ten times every day. Toning your muscles will also boost your orgasms and help you flex your muscles around your man during sex. He can tone up his muscles too, by putting a flannel over his erect penis, then raising and lowering it.

Bear in mind that asparagus and curry can both make urine taste unpleasant, whereas alcohol can help you keep the stream going for longer and lots of water will keep it weak enough to be more pleasant. If you want to get really kinky, you can change the colour of your urine; beetroot will turn it pink.

If you're willing to drink your man's urine, make sure you're in control so you don't choke or gag. Get him to start peeing then move under the stream to drink.

Urine is generally a sterile fluid. However, urine is not safe if someone has an infection, and it can contain bacteria. It can also contain minute quantities of HIV so it's best not to get too extreme unless you've both been tested.

Bukkake

What is it?

Bukkake is a Japanese term referring to showering a receiver – usually female – with sperm from one or more men. It's thought to have originated in Ancient Japan as a punishment for unfaithful women, who were publicly humiliated by being tied up while every man in town ejaculated all over them. Over time, it has moved to become a sexual practice, first shown in facial cum shot videos in the 1980s.

While the majority of men say that they prefer to come down a woman's throat, according to a poll by queendom.com, ten per cent like to ejaculate on their partner's body, and a further ten per cent like to come over her face.

In the same poll, 18 per cent of women said that they like ejaculate on their body and three per cent like it on their face. So if you like the idea of being a cum-queen, you're not the only one.

What to do if he asks for it?
Let's face it, very few women are going to be up for a bukkake session with multiple partners, so we're dealing with solo bukkake here. If you don't want him to come on your face, consider having a 'pearl necklace' instead, letting him ejaculate on your chest and neck. Apart from anything else, it's a great excuse not to swallow if you're not into that kind of thing.

What to do if you want it?
Start slowly, asking your man to come on your breasts, and work your way up. If he's game, you can experiment with different techniques. Ask him to aim the first blast towards your forehead, then try to cover your whole face with subsequent shots. He could even use his penis to rub the semen around your face. With 'smeared bukkake', you rub the ejaculate into your skin after he's come on you. Semen is thought to be good for the skin, so you'll be getting a facial in more ways than one.

Other hints and tips
Put your man on an 'ejaculation boosting' diet for ultimate bukkake. (It'll keep his prostate in shape, too.) The most

important nutrient for ejaculation is zinc, which is found in bananas and seafood (why do you think Casanova ate all those oysters?). The prostate needs ten times more zinc than any other organ in the body, but 90 per cent of men don't eat enough. Give him a zinc supplement of 15–45mg daily and you should notice an increase in the amount of semen he produces.

Lycopene (found in tomatoes), arginine (taken as a supplement of 500mg daily and 1,000mg 30–40 minutes prior to sexual activity) and beta-sitosterol (also taken as a supplement) can also boost the volume of ejaculate, while niacin promotes increased blood flow to all parts of his body, including the scrotum and testicles.

Tantric techniques can also increase the amount of ejaculate that he sprays on you. Get him to bring himself close to orgasm several times in a row before finally letting himself come. He can also increase the volume of semen by 'storing it up' for two or three days (after that, excess semen just comes out when he urinates).

Bear in mind that semen can hurt if it goes up your nose and cause alkaline burns if it gets in your eye, so make sure your man has good aim. A penis is capable of shooting semen anywhere from 12 to 24 inches, and the initial spurt of ejaculate travels at 28 miles per hour – faster than the world record for the 100 yard dash – so he'll need to keep firm control over himself.

Cross-dressing

What is it?

Cross-dressing involves deriving sexual pleasure from wearing clothes of the opposite sex. Contrary to popular belief, the vast majority of cross-dressers are heterosexual. While still taboo, it is becoming more socially acceptable, with public figures such as comedian Eddie Izzard 'out' as transvestites. Four per cent of men fantasise about cross-dressing according to *My Secret Garden Shed*.

Male cross-dressers often feel that women are pampered,

You've got to be kidding!

Of course, there's always the chance that you might meet someone really freaky. Here are some of the scarier fetishes out there; if you meet someone who asks for one of these, run a mile.

- Emetophilia: arousal from consuming vomit or being vomited on.
- Enema cocktail: Drinking the contents of a purged enema.
- Ederacinsim: Tearing out sexual organs from the roots.
- Meatotomy: Dilating the urethra with a medical

so wearing women's clothes makes them feel the same and escape from work stresses. Dr Pam Spurr says, 'Cross-dressing appeals to men as they can relax into the feminine role and be a completely different person; either appealing to a feminine side they already have or as completely different womanly persona altogether. It allows them to tinker and toy with make-up, accessories and fashion in a way that's not permitted to men by society. For most men there is less of a sexual element than simply a 'gender' element.'

dilating device; the urethra is stretched enough to accommodate a finger or penis.

- Hemotigolagnia: Arousal from used and bloody sanitary pads.
- Avisodomy: Breaking the neck of a bird then using the hole for sex.
- Mucophagy: Consuming mucous secretions (ie snot).
- Odontophilia: Arousal from tooth extraction.
- Scrotal infusion: Infusion of saline solution into the scrotal sack so that it enlarges.
- Infantilism: Dressing up as a baby for sexplay.

Source: Encyclopaedia of unusual sexual practices, *Brenda Love, Abacus*

What to do if he asks for it?

If you don't think that you could keep a straight face if your man wears a full stockings and suspenders combo, consider just swapping undies with him (or letting him wear your knickers; you don't have to wear his grungy pants). Don't give him your most expensive lingerie, though, you don't want it stretched beyond all recognition.

What to do if you want it?

Women have it slightly easier than men if they want to indulge in cross-dressing; wearing trousers or even boxers is pretty much accepted nowadays. You can even go full-on, *Nine and a Half Weeks* style, in the name of sexual experimentation and go out dressed as a man if the idea appeals and you're feeling brave.

If you want to get him – literally – into your pants, it may be a touch harder – but not that much. Most men are at least vaguely curious, and if you suggest swapping undies for a bit of fun when you're both a bit tipsy, he'll probably go along with it.

Other hints and tips

If the man you pull is seriously into cross-dressing, recommend that he pays a visit to transformation.co.uk. It has a host of clothing, fake breasts and even hormone treatments. They have an advisory service so that he can discuss his needs.

He wanted to be a woman: Julie's story

I met Miles at a party and we got on well so, when he asked me out on a date, I was really excited about it. I told all my mates about him and thought that it could lead to a relationship.

The evening went brilliantly; conversation flowed and he treated me to a fantastic dinner. I thought that he was gorgeous so, when he walked me home, I invited him in for 'coffee'.

Coffee became cuddling and cuddling became petting and soon our hands were straying all over each other's bodies. When I started rubbing his thigh, I was a bit confused. I was sure that I could feel a suspender belt. He noticed that I was perturbed, and blushingly explained that he hadn't expected us to end up in bed that night, but he liked the feeling of women's underwear and often wore it under his (manly) clothes.

I really liked him but the thought of seeing him in stockings and suspenders made me cringe. I made my excuses and he took the hint and left. Part of me regrets it; in all other ways, we got on brilliantly. But I just couldn't cope with the idea of a man in women's clothes.

Living out fantasies: yes or no – and if so, how?

It's not all fetish out there in casual-sex land. There's an awful lot of vanilla sex. And then there's fantasy; that stuff that you think about when you're doing the self-love thing or during sex. Having pervy thoughts doesn't mean that you're not getting enough. Indeed, it generally suggests the opposite. Your libido is high enough to make you horny most of the time, which has got to be a good thing.

So where do you draw the line between fantasy and reality? If you're going out and shagging the planet, then you may as well get the sex that you want. And while sometimes you may want to keep your erotic imaginings to yourself, sharing your thoughts with the person you're having sex with may help you reach new heights in your night of fun.

But how do you broach adding fantasies to your sex life? After all, it's hard enough learning what a new bloke wants in bed before you go adding masks, whipped cream or feathers into the equation.

One good way, if you've got a fuck-buddy thing going on, is to use the phone to introduce the subject, as the distance provided can help spare your blushes. Give the guy a call at an appropriate time; during a business meeting or while he's seeing another woman is less than ideal. Start by telling him that you've been thinking about him. One of the highest compliments you can pay a man is saying that you've masturbated about him. Men love it, and there are few things guaranteed to get him harder.

Use this to lead into your fantasy. 'I was thinking that, as you look so gorgeous in your leather trousers, it would be good for you to be an evil highwayman intent on stealing my honour.' Listen to his reaction carefully. If he's absorbed in what you're saying and making lots of affirmative noises like 'Yes,' and 'Go on,' then continue what you're saying. Make it clear that this is a fantasy rather than something you'd really like to happen, at least until you're sure that he's into the idea too.

If you're too shy to tell him what you think – and there's no need to be because if you know him well enough to fuck him, you know him well enough to talk about it – say it with text instead. Sending a seductive text message can be a great way to share your fantasies (as long as you're sure he won't show his mates – unless that's part of your fantasy). Start with an open-ended question such as 'I'm wearing a French maid's outfit. You've just walked in and think I look irresistible. What do you do?' Keep things tame at first and get progressively ruder if he likes your idea.

Another good trick, if it's a guy you have sex with fairly regularly, is to write him a pervy fantasy and email it to him (previous warnings about email discretion taken into account, of course).

If you're confident enough to talk about your fantasies face to face, one of the easiest ways to introduce them is while you're having sex. You've both got all those lust chemicals floating through your body, which are great for masking embarrassment. Again, make sure you know the man's not going to be turned off by your fantasies, as spoiling the mood is the last thing you want to do. But if you know that he's not freaked out by the idea of submitting to the will of a stranger or playing doctor, incorporate it into proceedings, whether verbally or with props.

A word of warning: no matter how casual your relationship is, be very sure that your bloke is emotionally secure before you mention other people, either as an addition to your fantasy sex, or in his place. While you may dream about some Hollywood idol, even the most blasé guy has an ego, and it's not going to do you any favours if he thinks that he's not enough for you. Similarly, calling him by someone else's name is liable to make him (and his manhood) sulk.

Most importantly, remember that fantasy and reality are not the same thing, so you should never feel obliged to live something out unless you both want to. Don't feel pressured by anyone into doing something you'd rather keep as a fantasy and, conversely, don't try to make him do anything that he doesn't want to. It may only be casual sex but consent is still all-important.

Chapter 6

The Morning After

You've had your wicked way with some fit bloke. Assuming that he hasn't sneaked out in the middle of the night – or you have – you now face the joys of the morning after.

Even the most laid-back woman can feel uncomfortable when she's faced with the person she was begging for more a few hours earlier. You may want to see him again, but have no idea how to mention it. You might want to escape the swamp-monster from hell (and swear off tequila for life). Or you might find yourself in one of many nightmare scenarios: unable to get out of a locked house; late for work and looking dreadful; realising your purse has vanished along with the bloke; or, heaven forbid, lying in a wet patch that reminds you that the condom split last night.

Goodbye and thank you

Depending on where you are and what you want, the way you part will vary. Some of the most common scenarios are as follows:

Scenario one

Location: Your place

Your attitude: 'Let's do that again'

His attitude: Non-commital

How to behave: If you're not sure whether he's into you or not (regardless of how far into you he got last night) then dignity is all-important. Say that you're making yourself breakfast and ask if he'd like some. That way, if he wants to escape, he can make his excuses and you'll know where you stand. Let him go. Life's too short to chase people who aren't interested.

If he decides to stay for breakfast, it's an indication that he likes you (or he might just be hungry). Do the 'making conversation' thing without being too heavy (eg, avoid asking 'So where's our relationship going?'). Then kick him out. Even if it's a weekend. There's something in the old 'leave him wanting more' thing. Make sure that you've exchanged phone numbers first, though; there's such a thing as being too elusive.

One of the best ways to get a guy's number is to ask him to text you from his phone; that way you can be sure that he doesn't give you a fake number, or scrawl it so illegibly that you can never get hold of him again. That said, he should be calling you if you made the first move ...

Scenario two

Location: Your place

Your attitude: 'Let's do that again'

His attitude: Get me out of here right now

How to behave: If he's coming up with excuses about early meetings/squash games then let him go. He's clearly a one-night stand merchant. Don't waste time trying to get his number. He'll never answer your calls anyway. Just enjoy the night for what it was.

Scenario three

Location: Your place

Your attitude: 'I'm never drinking again!'

His attitude: But I love you

How to behave: Tell him your mum's on her way over, or that you've got to go to work, even if you don't have to. You can always leave the house and walk around the block a few times until he's safely out of the way (if he sees you sneaking back, tell him you forgot an important folder).

If he already knows that you don't have work, suggest going out for breakfast as you've got nothing in the house. Once he's out of the house, it's much easier to ditch him. But have breakfast with him first unless he was actually nasty; you don't want to be mean.

NB: Never leave an over-keen man in the house and go to work; you could well return to find him waiting for you. And your pet rabbit in a saucepan.

Scenario four

Location: His place

Your attitude: 'Let's do that again'

His attitude: Non-commital

How to behave: Ask if you can have a coffee. If he offers you breakfast, too, then he's clearly interested. If he grunts something about being out of milk, he wants you to leave. But if he offers to take you out for breakfast, don't panic. Unlike women, men won't tend to go for the 'let her down gently' route, so it's an indication that he enjoys your company. After breakfast, leave (having first exchanged numbers), and wait for him to call. Or rather, go out partying and, if he rings, fab. If not, let it go.

Scenario five

Location: His place

Your attitude: 'Let's do that again'

His attitude: You've got to go, my mum's due any minute.

How to behave: Smile graciously and leave immediately. He wanted a one-nighter and nothing more. The only way to keep your dignity is to brazen it out.

Scenario six

Location: His place

Your attitude: 'I'm never drinking again!'

His attitude: But I love you

How to behave: Make your excuses and leave. If he asks for your number, say, 'Sorry, I don't think that this should happen again'. You can soften the blow by adding, 'I realised I'm not over my ex,' if you feel so inclined.

Scenario seven

Location: Anywhere

Your attitude: 'Let's do that again'

His attitude: 'Let's do that again'

How to behave: Do it again. Duh!

Morning-after monstrosities

There are times when things don't go exactly to plan. Indeed, the golden rule is that anything can happen when you're shagging around. Cultivate an aura of 'Whatever,' and you'll always look like you're handling things, even if you're trembling inside.

His ex turned up: Louise's story

I'd been seeing Tony for a couple of weeks; nothing serious, as we were both getting over messy break-ups. One night, I'd done a sexy strip for him and things were just getting interesting when there was a loud knocking at the door. First of all he ignored it but, when it continued for ten minutes, he went downstairs, leaving me lying under the covers, naked and horny.

I heard shouting and realised that it was his ex-girlfriend. She'd just found out he'd cheated on her (not with me) and had come round to have it out with him. The shouting continued for a while, and I huddled under the covers, terrified that she'd come storming upstairs. I hadn't done anything wrong, but I still felt guilty and, after a while, decided to get dressed, as I felt too vulnerable naked.

Then, I heard her say 'Well, get her down here then!' Tony came upstairs and explained that Celia, his ex, wanted to tell me what he'd done. He'd already told me he'd cheated on her, but I figured that if that was what she wanted, I'd do as she asked.

I went downstairs, shaking slightly, and sat opposite her. She said 'I know this is weird,' and for a while we made small talk – but soon, she was rowing with Tony again, this time saying, 'I bet you never knew that about him!' at pointed intervals. I didn't know what to do. I felt bad for her; Tony was just a fling for me, but it was obvious that they still had deep feelings for each other. I didn't have enough money for a cab and it was late at night, so I couldn't even leave.

Eventually, she stormed off and Tony followed her. I slept in his bed, alone, horrified at what had just happened. Needless to say, I didn't see him again.

Common nightmare scenarios are as follows:

Forgetting the guy's name

You know how it is; meet some bloke, get chatting, go back to his place, have fun – and then realise you have no idea what he's called. It seems rude to ask someone's name after you've made the beast with two backs, so you need to get sneaky.

If you're alone in his room, try to find his wallet to see if there's a business card inside. Be wary if there's only one though: it could belong to someone else he met (make sure you don't get caught or he'll think you're nicking his cash). Or look at the envelopes of any letters addressed to him, as they may also help. Alternatively, ask him for his number (assuming you want to see him again) and, as he's writing, say 'Oh, and can you put your name above it? I don't want to mix your number up with any business numbers.'

If you're really brave, you can go for the brazen approach of 'Look, last night was incredible but I was so drunk that I utterly forgot your name. I'm [blah]. Who are you?' If you're lucky, he'll have forgotten your name, too, and be grateful that you've broached the issue. Either that, or he'll be so offended that you never see him again.

Sneaky but sweet: Jon's story

My top tip is for that delicate situation when you wake up and have no idea of the identity of the person lying next to you, is to quite simply get out of bed, go and make them breakfast (doesn't have to be fancy, a cup of coffee will do) and while you are there try and track down some of their mail to get their name. Not only do you score points for knowing their name (when they might not know yours) but you will forever be the lovely fella/lass who made them breakfast after your casual encounter.

This approach is not 100 per cent foolproof, however. They may be some sort of compulsive tidy person and have no mail lying around. If so, I'm afraid you are out of luck. Just try not to make a mess before leaving, OK?

Take extra care if they do not live alone. Having to call them (insert your own term of endearment here) repeatedly until you can escape is better than calling them by their flatmate's name because you got the wrong mail. Also, bumping into said flatmate while making breakfast may give rise to some awkward questions, which you obviously cannot fully answer. Nevertheless, if you are lucky (like I was) then this approach will avoid the awkward impasse that you find yourself in and may even get you an improved, sober, repeat performance of the previous night's proceedings.

Waking up in an unfamiliar bed on a work-day, and have no change of clothes or make-up

As long as you have your 'Brief Encounter Kit' with you, this one's relatively easy to deal with. However, if you've forgotten it, never fear. The contents of the average man's bathroom can be used to make yourself look at least vaguely presentable. Men today spend more on grooming than ever before, so you may get lucky and find he has posher toiletries than you do. If not, get creative.

Start by hanging up your clothes in the bathroom while you're having a shower. The steam will help creases drop out and get rid of the smell of cigarette smoke.

Vaseline is ace as a multi-purpose product: slick it over your lips, cheeks and eyelids to give a 'barely there' make-up look. If you rub a tiny amount between your fingers then you can rub it on your eyelashes as surrogate mascara, too. That said, you may want to avoid the Vaseline if the tub is sitting next to a guy's bed and looking, err, used.

If you've got a lipstick stowed in your bag, that can double as blusher. And if the bloke has some talcum powder in the bathroom, it can double as face powder (but only use a tiny amount or you'll look like a vampire). OK, you won't look quite as good as you do with your full make-up kit to work with, but looking vaguely groomed will help you carry off the 'Of course I didn't go back to a stranger's house and spend all night fucking' line with suitable indignation.

Getting up after he's gone to work and realising that he's inadvertently locked you in
This one is more common than you may think; if his front door is one that locks from the outside with a key,

then it's a distinct possibility. It's happened to about five of my friends. To start with, give the guy a call, if you have his mobile number, so he can either tell you where the key is or come back to let you out.

If you don't have his number, look around for a key for the door, If that fails, look for alternative exits. There may be a back door that you can get out through. If there's no alternative door, you're on to windows. Pick the biggest one possible; you don't want to get stuck – it's unflattering as well as difficult to explain to the police.

If there are window locks, and you can't find the key, you're onto the most extreme option; smash a window, put a load of towels around the broken glass bits and climb out (assuming you're on the ground floor rather than in a penthouse flat). But avoid this if you possibly can; it's not likely to make a bloke want to sleep with you again and you could end up getting cut.

Getting out of his flat and realising you have no idea where you are
Again, if you've got your 'Brief Encounter Kit', you're laughing. Just look at the street name then look in your street map. From there, you can figure out a way home.

Failing that, head for the largest street you can see, and keep an eye out for bus stops. They'll usually have a sign ponting to the centre of town so you can get your bearings.

Some really slick mobile phones have global positioning systems (GPS) and can tell you where you are, so it's worth checking whether your phone knows more than you do. Then again, you could just look for a taxi and ask the driver to take you to the nearest public transport stop.

Sexually Transmitted Infections

While condoms are generally speaking pretty reliable, sometimes they split. And sometimes you're too drunk to use them (please realise that it's just not a risk worth taking; how hard is it to get a man into a small bit of rubber that could save both your lives, after all?). And then there are times when, despite practising safer sex, your bits start itching.

Any exchange of bodily fluids is potentially risky, and for infections such as herpes and genital warts, even skin-to-skin contact can be a risk. In total, there are at least 25 infections and infestations that are transmissible through sex, so if you're having sex of any kind, you could be unlucky and catch the lurgy.

A whopping one in ten people have a Sexually Transmitted Infection (STI) at any one time, and three quarters of a million people are diagnosed with an STI in the UK very year. Genital warts is the most common STI in the United States. The US Center for Disease Control estimates that 1 million new cases of genital herpes occur each year with about 45 million Americans currently infected with herpes. Like it or not, STIs are here to stay. If you think you've got one, or are worried about your bits in any way at all, get to a doctors. In the UK you can get health information outside surgery times by telephoning NHS Direct on 0845 4647 or visit nhsdirect.nhs.uk. If you live in Scotland, visit the Health Education Board for Scotland's HEBSWEB at hebs.org.uk.

A good vixen should get tested every year regardless of condom usage; most things can be easily treated if they're caught early enough, and it's better to be safe than sorry. If you go with a friend, and plan to go out somewhere fun afterwards, it's a lot less intimidating. You've also got someone's hand to hold when you're waiting for the result and can support each other if anything nasty does surface.

If you find out you have an STI, you should tell previous partners so that they can check whether they're infected and, if so, have the disease properly diagnosed and treated. (If need be, UK STI clinics can tell your exes anonymously.)

And you should obviously tell anyone you want to have sex with or abstain until the infection has gone away. Apart from anything else, you're unlikely to want to have sex. As a general guide, any of the following should be taken as warning signs:

- Pain or a burning feeling when you pee.
- Pain when you have sex.
- Peeing more often than usual.
- Rash or irritation around the vagina or anus.

- Sores, warts or blisters around the genital area.
- Unusual vaginal discharge.

Thrush

Thrush isn't always considered to be a sexually transmitted infection; it's in all of us at times, but can get a chance to flourish if you are pregnant, wear tight jeans or nylon underwear, have diabetes, are stressed, anaemic or your immune system is suppressed, you are on the pill, taking certain antibiotics or having unprotected sex with someone with thrush. Around 75 per cent of women will get it at some stage or other, and it's easily treated with creams, pessaries or an oral treatment.

Symptoms include itching and irritation around vagina or anus, pain during sex or urination and thick cheesy discharge from the vagina. And it's not just the usual itching bits; you can also get oral thrush, which amounts to a sore and possibly bleeding or lumpy tongue. Again, this is easily treated with special medicated pastilles.

The only risks from thrush are the inherent nastiness of the symptoms, but it's worth treating as soon as you detect it as it can put your bits out of action by making them too sore for sex.

Chlamydia

One of the most common STIs around today, the problem with chlamydia is that it's frequently devoid of any symptoms at all. There are many different varieties of it and it is transmissible and contractible even if you're not showing symptoms. At least 50 per cent of chlamydia is asymptomatic but, if you do show symptoms, it could be bleeding between periods, burning pain when you pee, unusual discharge from your vagina, pain and/or bleeding during or after sex, itching and burning around your vagina, lower abdominal pain and (rarely) fever.

If left to its own devices, it can damage your reproductive organs and lead to infertility and pelvic inflammatory disease (PID). There's also thought to be an increased risk of cervical cancer with type G chlamydia and, if you're pregnant, you risk passing the disease on to the baby during birth, causing infections in its eyes, ears, lungs and genitals.

Genital warts
Also known as venereal sarts and condyloma, genital warts are caused by the human papilloma virus (HPV), of which there are over one hundred varieties, some of which particularly like the genital area. The symptoms are gloriously nasty; small, soft growths that are white, pink or brown and can look like cauliflowers (no, not the same size, stop panicking) or be flat. You can feel them with your fingers – just wash your hands afterwards.

Many people don't show any symptoms of genital warts other than the warts themselves. Scarily, even without the warts, you may have the virus that causes them, and thus be able to give them to other people. If you do have warts, you may be more susceptible to other infections. Some strains of the HPV virus that cause warts can cause cervical cancer.

When detected early, cervical cancer is treatable, so make sure you go for your regular smear tests so any signs of its presence can be detected as soon as possible. Warts are treated by being burned off (with chemicals rather than a big flame), frozen off, or by special creams applied regularly, usually from home.

Pubic lice and scabies

Remember the annoyance that was nits when you were a kid? Imagine the same thing but in your pubes; not nice at all. Commonly known as crabs, pubic lice are annoying little insects that live on your body and are visible to the naked eye. Symptoms include blisters and bumps, itching, crusting and redness from scratching. And if you scratch – which, let's face it, you're going to – it can open the skin surface and increase your risk of infection with other STIs.

Pubic lice are treated in a similar way to nits; a solution they hate is applied from your head to the tip of your toes. You have to wash all your bedding too, so that you don't get re-infected.

Trichomonas

One of the hardest STIs to pronounce, trichomonas is sometimes called 'trich' or 'TV'. It's caused by a tiny parasite found in the vagina and urethra. Like chlamydia, there are often very few symptoms and it is sometimes discovered during a routine cervical smear. However, signs to watch out for are an increase in vaginal discharge, which may also become thinner, frothy or yellow/green/grey in colour and develop a musty fishy smell. Sex may be painful, as may peeing. And your bits could be sore and inflamed. On the plus side, there's no known lasting damage and a dose of antibiotics will soon sort you out.

Syphilis
It went out of fashion for a while but now, sadly, syphilis is back with a vengeance. Caused by the bacteria treponema palladium, it produces symptoms that occur in stages starting anywhere from 10 to 90 days after contraction. Syphilis is highly infections for a full two years after you catch it.

In stage one, you'll usually just get sores (firm, round and often painless) – or nothing at all. By stage two, you can add a sore throat, swollen glands, white patches in the mouth, acne-like warts in the groin area, fever, hair falling out in patches from infected areas, pox-like pus-filled bumps on the hands, feet and palms (possibly where the 'hairs on the palm of your hand from excessive masturbation' myth came from) and scales on your body – or nothing at all.

Stage three can be very serious and show up years later. It often starts to affect internal organs; the blood vessels, brain, bones, eyes, heart, joints, liver and nerves, which is why it's all important to get to the doctors as soon as you suspect there's anything wrong down below.

Risks of syphilis (as if the symptoms weren't bad enough) include blindness, dementia, paralysis, infertility and infection of babies if you're pregnant. Your baby could get anaemia, jaundice, bloody infectious patches, skin sores, a swollen liver or could even be stillborn. But if you get to the doctors the second you suspect it, it can be easily treated with antibiotics. You know what to do …

Gonorrhoea
The hardest to spell of all the STIs, gonorrhoea is a bacterium that grows and multiplies quickly in warm, moist areas (like your vag) and there are over six hundred different strains of it to choose from. It can affect the urethra, vagina, cervix, anus, throat, joints and eyes. Symptoms, if you get any, include painful joints, a mild sore throat or slight fever, burning pain when you pee, tenderness during sex (no, that doesn't mean a man will start crooning 'Unchained Melody' in your ear), pain in your bowels, a rash on the palms, rectal discomfort and a thick green/yellow discharge.

Risks include blood poisoning (gonoccocal septicaemia), brain damage, ectopic pregnancy, heart damage (endocarditis), infertility and pelvic inflammatory disease

(PID). And if you are pregnant, your baby could develop an eye infection that can lead to blindness if not treated.

Again, it's easily treated by a doctor with a quick dose of pills, so get it sorted before it gets serious.

Herpes
Caused by a virus, type one herpes (herpes simplex virus, HSV 1), is from the same group that causes chicken pox and is referred to as oral herpes. Remember, never let a man with a cold-sore go down on you – or do anything to you, frankly – as you could get herpes. Genital and oral herpes are different things, but type one herpes is responsible for 40 per cent of all genital herpes, meaning that it was transmitted through oral sex.

Type two herpes is less common and is known as genital herpes. That said, up to one in twelve people in the UK have genital herpes, so it's still pretty damned common. Symptoms usually appear between two and twelve days after contraction, and can disappear and reappear. You'll get blisters and sores in oral (type one herpes) and genital (type two herpes) areas. You could also feel shattered and flu-ish, with a fever.

In addition to the general mankiness of the symptoms, herpes can infect babies during delivery resulting in possible mental retardation and susceptibility to other diseases, or even death. It's incurable, but alternative and traditional medicine can both help ease the symptoms.

HIV and AIDS

The really scary one; HIV is the abbreviation for human immunodeficiency virus, and AIDS is acquired immunodeficiency syndrome. You can have HIV without having AIDS. Tragically, it's currently incurable, although many researchers are working on both treatments and vaccines, and new drug treatments offer hope to sufferers, often prolonging and improving their lives.

Since the first cases surfaced in 1981 AIDS has killed more than 22 million people throughout the world, and over 36 million people are today living with HIV.

Initial symptoms of HIV infection are similar to flu and usually last three to fourteen days and then go away. Even while the symptoms are not evident, the virus is still multiplying in the body and the sufferer can spread the virus to others. Within several months of HIV infection there may be repeated episodes of flu-like symptoms. Glands or lymph nodes can become swollen in the early stages of HIV infection; check them by feeling in the neck and groin with your fingers. Other early symptoms include abdominal pain, diarrhoea, herpes zoster, night sweats, oral thrush, skin rashes and tiredness. All of these symptoms can also be caused by other conditions, so may not be linked to your sex life, particularly if you've been out partying heavily.

After that, an average period of five to seven years will pass without another sign of HIV infection, although this delay can range from a few months to more than fifteen years. At this later stage, symptoms can include: arthritis; dermatitis; frequent and severe herpes infections causing sores on genitals, anus and mouth; mental impairment; mild weight loss; inflammation of various internal organs; painful nerve disease; skin rashes; yeast infections; personality changes; pneumonia; and short-term memory loss.

Onset of full-blown AIDS is characterised by the appearance of other opportunistic infections that take hold because the immune system is weakened. HIV and AIDS may involve virtually every organ in the body, so many other conditions may be mistaken for them, including cancer, pneumonia, toxoplasmosis of the brain and tuberculosis. It can also cause chronically active HIV infection (HIV wasting syndrome). AIDS can be passed to babies during pregnancy or through birth and also during breast-feeding.

The earlier HIV is caught, the better your prognosis will be, so get yourself tested on a regular basis to ensure that you are in the best position to handle it, should the worst happen. And use a condom when you shag, so that it doesn't.

It wasn't worth the risk: Rosie's story

Last year I woke up after my work Christmas party next to Tim, the most gorgeous boy in the entire company. We ended up spending the weekend together, walking in the park, drinking lots of wine, eating delicious food and having lots of sex. Mostly we had oral sex, because we didn't have a condom (I was on the pill but better to be safe …). He slipped his cock into me without a condom for maybe five tantalising seconds at one point and God, I was aching for it to stay in for longer, but we behaved and I didn't think much else about it.

On Monday morning I staggered into work, dazed with lack of sleep and too much red wine. He had gone back to the other side of the country (he worked in one of our regional offices and I was based in London) and we had left it that he'd call me next time he was in the area. Oh, I was the kittycat who'd had the cream alright; all day I beamed and gazed out of the window remembering … and then something he'd said came back to me. He had, in the past, used drugs intravenously. And he had been inside me, unprotected.

I started thinking about HIV, about how easily it can be caught, how easily it can be spread. I tried to push these thoughts to the back of my mind but they ate away at me every day. I should have just called and asked him if there was any risk but I just couldn't bring myself to have the conversation.

In the end I went to the local clap clinic, but they explained that you have to wait for three months after the 'incident' for the test to be accurate. It was hell. Three months is a really long time to wait for anything but if the results are going to affect how long you might live for, whether you will have children or not, whether you might have a lifetime of medication to look forward to, it is truly awful.

Tim had started seeing someone else but that barely registered; I couldn't think about seeing anyone until I knew. As the date became closer, though, I started to feel more relaxed about it; there was nothing I could do, I just had to wait.

Then I fell in love. I didn't feel I could sleep with my new boyfriend without telling him first, I couldn't take the risk of the condom splitting and infecting him too. My insides were crumbling as I told him, I felt so ashamed. Luckily he was incredibly supportive and when I had the test (the results came back negative) he was the first person I told.

We're still together now but I know that, if I'm ever single again, I will never take the risk of casual sex without a condom. It is simply not worth it.

Chapter 7

The Four-letter Word

If you've read every page so far then you should know pretty much everything there is to know about casual sex. If you skipped the bit on STIs, go back and read it. Shagging around is fine but being a reckless venereal-disease spreader gives all casual sex devotees a bad name. No, really. You are banned from reading beyond this point until you read the STI bit.

OK, assuming you've done as you're told, you'll know everything there is to know about casual sex. Except. Well, there's that love thing. Now you may be a sophisticated urban chick, and you may feel quite capable of having sex without emotion, but it happens to the best of us. After all, casual sex is lovely but the whole love, marriage and babies thing can be pretty compelling.

Before you commit yourself — which 'I love you' kind of does — think about whether you're ready for a relationship. Are you still hung up on an ex? Can you guarantee (as much as anyone ever can) that you'll be faithful? Have you talked about the things that you feel are important, be it religion, politics or whatever other issues matter most to you? Would you be happy to meet his folks and introduce him to yours? (OK, not happy — it's a bloody nightmare — but at least not object to it too much.) And has he passed your mental 'tick-list' (or indeed, the positive visualisation list you wrote having read Chapter 3)?

Other things to check are:

Do you like him as much as you fancy him?
If not, it's probably just lust. Sorry, darling.

Do your friends like him?
It's not all-important — after all, you're dating him, not them — but if your mates glaze over when you mention his name or rapidly change the subject, they may see something that your love-chemical induced haze has hidden from your view. Ask them what the problem is. Your mates know you pretty well, and won't want to see you with an idiot. Then again, they could just be glazing over because you've turned into a love-struck bore. You've got three months, and then you have to turn back into a normal person, OK?

Do you have similar interests?
Boring as it sounds, people with similar interests tend to have more successful relationships than people who don't.

Do you both have separate social lives?
Love is great but not to the exclusion of everyone else. Make sure you keep on having a life outside your relationship. Otherwise you'll just get boring.

It may sound cold, but analyse why you feel the way you do. Sometimes, you can convince yourself that you're falling in love when, actually, you're just familiar with each other. And don't forget about all those chemicals that flood your body when you have sex, either. Many a smart woman has mistaken lust for love, and lived to regret it.

I thought it was love: Anna's story

An ex and I spent two years pretending that we were having a relationship when really we were just repeatedly having casual sex. The thing I've learned is that you should recognise when sex is casual sex, and keep it as such.

If, after all that, you really do think you're falling in love, take it slowly. Consider whether the bloke feels the same way. If he doesn't, don't waste time trying to convince him. At best, you'll get a half-hearted excuse of a relationship where you have to make all the running — and you're worth more than that.

If you think he may feel the same way, you should still act with caution. As a general rule, wait for at least three dates *after* you think you're falling for a guy before you actually tell him. With any luck, he'll beat you to it so you'll never have to worry about whether he just 'said it back' so that you didn't stop sleeping with him.

If he doesn't act first, start slowly. Go for 'I really like you', well before you dive in with 'I love you and have been picturing the house with roses round the door and our kids will be called Jane and John and we'll have a dog and we'll go on holiday to the beach and …' You get the picture.

If you're right, and he does feel the same way then, with any luck, he'll say it back and you can fade into a rose-tinted glow. (But don't hang up that condom quite yet; you both need to get tested for all STIs before you go for bareback bonking. Love doesn't protect against STIs.)

If he doesn't say it back, give him another couple of dates. It may be that you shocked him or that he needs time to think. If he still doesn't say it back, sorry darling, but you should dump him. You'll only fall more in love the longer you stay with him, and that way leads to heartbreak.

Of course, it may be that you can sleep around for years and still not meet Mr Right. And fair enough. With good friends and good sex, you can have a perfectly happy life – and you'll certainly have to compromise less. The grass genuinely is greener on the other side (or, more to the point, the grass is longer because the lazy bastard you've hooked up with spends all his time watching TV and never gets round to mowing it).

It may seem like relationships are fab, and they can be, but you come into this life alone, and you leave it alone. The point is to enjoy the time that you have got. And whether you have a billion brief encounters or settle into marital bliss, with the right attitude (and fabulous shoes) you'll be sure to have the time of your life.

Sex Up your Life

Other Useful Resources

Brilliant books

Dr Pam Spurr has a range of essential guides to love, sex and relationships. Some favourites include:

The Break-up Survival Kit – Emotional Rescue for the Newly Single
The Dating Survival Guide – The Ten Top Tactics for Total Success!
Sex, Guys & Chocolate – Your Essential Guide to Lust, Love & Life!

They are published by Robson Books and are available from amazon.co.uk and all good bookstores.

Flic Everett is another fab sex writer, who advised on the UK TV series *Sex Tips for Girls*. Her book of the same name, published by Channel 4 Books, is well worth a read. Or set your inner vixen free with *How to Be a Sex Goddess* (Carlton).

Erin Kelly's book, *Searching for Sex in the City: How to Find Your Mr Big* (Ebury Press) is a witty guide to finding that perfect person (and losing any idiots).

And finally, there's *The Big Bang* by Emma Taylor and Lorelei Sharke (or, as they're more commonly known, Em and Lo). Packed with info on almost every sexual practice you can imagine, this is a sharp and entertaining read (Hodder).

Confidence-boosters

Peta Heskell knows everything there is to know about flirting; so much, in fact, that she runs courses on it. And, let's face it, the people there are more than likely to be single so it's a good pulling opportunity, too. See flirt-coach.com for details.

If you want some sexy pictures, you need Sauce. Describing her service as 'stylish intimate photography for women', Sauce creates images of you to enchant the object of your desires. Trust me, having one of them on your wall will make conquests desperate to rip your clothes off. Well worth a trip to London. See sauce-goddess.co.uk.

If you want to know how to remove your clothes in the most seductive way, sign up for a course at the London School of Striptease. Fabulous tutor Jo King has a chatty style and friendly demeanour that makes even the shyest woman feel relaxed. See lsos.co.uk. You can even invest in your very own pole-dancing pole, thanks to mypole.co.uk. Don't worry if you're outside the UK; it has links to over-seas suppliers too.

If you want a great excuse to get glammed up, try cakenyc.com or cakelondon.com. These are sexy events for women, where you can generally get a lap-dance from foxy male and female performers, and enjoy your sexuality in a relaxed and safe environment.

Two organisers of swinging events are feverparties.com, who have useful info on their website for newbies; and loungeparties.com, who arrange parties for attractive couples and bi girls, generally in London. No sex happens at the events, instead you can meet like-minded people and arrange your own entertainments. For dogging events and parties, try ukrudegirl.com.

A US site filled with quality erotic stories is cleansheets.com. And don't forget cliterati.co.uk, which I describe under 'also by the author'.

Sexy presents

Want some chocolate body paint that actually tastes nice? Visit sensualise.co.uk. Its body paint isn't just made from the best Belgian chocolate. It also comes in gorgeous glass bottles shaped like male or female torsos and adds class to any boudoir.

ooshka.com has all those other essential ingredients to make your boudoir (and lingerie drawer) as classy as it can be. It delivers to the UK and Australia. Or check out sextoys. co.uk or lovehoney.co.uk, which delivers to numerous locations all over the world including Europe, New Zealand, Australia, Hong Kong and Japan.

Fab US sex shop goodvibes.com offers workshops,

seminars and even has an antique vibrator museum. Meanwhile evesgarden.com has everything you could possibly want to buy to use in the bedroom (or wherever). It's been going since 1974, which gives you an idea of how forward-thinking the team is.

Advice

For sexual health advice – and a terrifying STI picture gallery that will have you reaching for your condoms – visit willyworries.com. By buying *Brief Encounters*, you're supporting it as I'm making a donation to the foundation for every copy sold. However, do your own bit by signing up to the site as a paying member, too.

And for brilliant advice on sex and disability, visit outsiders.org.uk. It helps disabled people increase their confidence and find new friends and partners.

One of the most inspirational sex researchers ever, Nancy Friday, wrote *My Secret Garden*, the book that showed women really do have sexual fantasies. She's subsequently written about mother/daughter relationships, jealousy and numerous angles on the whole sexual fantasy thing. A true pioneer, her website is nancyfriday.com.

The Sexuality Information and Education Council of the United States – siecus.org – offers a national voice for sexuality education, sexual health and sexual rights. Academic but full of useful information.

scarleteen.com is designed for teenagers but suitable

for adults too: honest, interesting and detailed information about every aspect of sex and relationships.

Also by the author

Founded by me, Emily Dubberley, Cliterati is crammed with sexy stories designed to help women get off; perfect for those solo nights in (or reading to your conquest as alternative foreplay!). Anyone can add a story, as long as it's consensual and over-age. Over 2,000 to choose from and they're all free. The cliterati shop sells sex toys, lingerie and other sensual gifts worldwide. See cliterati.co.uk and cliteratishop.co.uk.

Scarlet Magazine, which I edit, is a mag with a real women's sense of humour. It includes feisty features, erotic pictures and hot stories. Subscribe at scarletmagazine.co.uk or find it in all good newsagents.

The *Lovers' Guide* videos, *Sexual Positions*, *Sexplay* and *Seven Keys to Complete Satisfaction*, offer advice in a sexy and informative format. They are available from all good video stores.

The *Lovers' Guide* 'Lovemaking Deck' (Connections) comprises 52 cards, each with a different sexual position to try, along with the advantages and disadvantages of them all. Available from all good bookstores.

Things a Woman Should Know About Seduction (Prion Books) is crammed with seduction tips from Hollywood screen icons and classic seductresses, from Mae West to Mata Hari, Cleopatra to Kylie. Available from all good bookstores.

References

Allison, Sadie (2001) *Tickle your fancy: A Woman's Guide to Sexual Self Pleasure* (Tickle Kitty Press)

Dodson, Betty (1987) *Sex for One: The Joy of Selfloving* (Harmony Books)

Eiseman, Leatrice (2000) *Colours For Your Every Mood* (Capital Books)

Friday, Nancy (2001) *My Secret Garden* (Quartet Books Ltd)

Love, Brenda (1995) *Encyclopaedia of Unusual Sexual Practices* (Abacus)

Reage, Pauline (1972) *The Story of O* (Corgi Adult)

Sacher-Masoch, Leopold Von (1990) *Venus in Furs* (Blast Books)

Scott, Paul (ed) (2002) *My Secret Garden Shed* (Nexus)

Pease, Allen and Barbara (2002) *Why Men Lie and Women Cry* (Orion Books)

About the Author

Emily Dubberley is the editor of *Scarlet*, the sex magazine for women who get what they want. She is the founder of cliterati.co.uk, has written three Lovers' Guide videos, and edited the *Lovers' Guide* magazine and website, loversguide.com. She has written for numerous magazines and newspapers including the *Guardian, Glamour* and *More*. She has also written SMS sex tips for various clients, has several regular radio slots and has appeared on TV shows including *Richard and Judy* and *Channel Four News*. She's reviewed over 200 sex toys in the last year alone. Her personal website is dubberley.com.

Vaginas
An Owner's Manual
Dr. Carol Livoti and Elizabeth Topp

'This is a book that every woman should own. It is as
entertaining as it is informative. Even your best
girlfriends can't give you this kind of advice.'
Candace Bushnell, author of *Sex and the City*

Dynamic mother–daughter team Dr. Carol Livoti and Elizabeth
Topp demystify the female anatomy and discuss everything a
woman needs to know about her reproductive system.

The authors describe each part of the female anatomy and how
it fits together, and offer advice on how to maintain reproductive
and genital health – from first period to beyond menopause.
Giving an overview of what to expect from medical consultations,
they also explain contraceptive options and abortion, STDs,
pregnancy and some of the most common gynaecological problems.

Easy-to-read and peppered with entertaining anecdotes from
Dr. Livoti's extensive career, this book is certain to become a classic
for women of all ages.

'A fabulous resource for the undiscovered country. Talk
about vagina friendly books! Got Vagina? Read this book.'
Eve Ensler, author of *The Vagina Monologues*

'Demystifies everything that should be demystified
and celebrates what should be celebrated.'
Naomi Wolf, author of *The Beauty Myth*

Non-fiction: Health
1-904132-64-2
£10.99